GOD'S REACH

BOOKS BY GLENN CLARK

What Would Jesus Do?

A Man's Reach

The Way, the Truth and the Life

I Will Lift Up Mine Eyes

The Soul's Sincere Desire

How To Find Health Through Prayer

Two or Three Gathered Together

Fishers of Men

Water of Life

Manual of the Short Story Art

The World's Greatest Debate

GOD'S REACH

BY

GLENN CLARK

Author of

"WHAT WOULD JESUS DO?"

"I WILL LIFT UP MINE EYES"

MACALESTER PARK PUBLISHING COMPANY

ST. PAUL   MINNESOTA

GOD'S REACH

Copyright 1951

By MACALESTER PARK PUBLISHING COMPANY

Published and distributed in The United States of America by Macalester Park Publishing Company, 1571 Grand Avenue, St. Paul 5, Minnesota.

ACKNOWLEDGMENTS

The author expresses his heartfelt gratitude for the precious assistance in the preparation of this manuscript rendered by Mildred Leisher, Ina Leith-ead, Grace Peterson, Franz Aust, Glen Stowe, Marcia Brown, Roberta Fletcher and Virginia and Miles Clark.

Grateful acknowledgment is made to the following authors and publishers for permission to quote from their books:

Vera Stanley Alder, author of *The Fifth Dimension and The Future of Mankind,* published by Rider & Company, London, England.

Gandhi, author of *Gandhi's Letters to a Disciple,* published by Harper and Brothers, New York.

Eastman, author of *Don't Pity the Animals in the Zoo,* from *The Readers' Digest,* Pleasantville, New York.

Contents

Part IV *Adventuring in the Higher Dimensions*

FOREWORD TO PART I

When in all history has there been a greater amassing of knowledge of man and the universe than in these last fifty years? Through psychiatry nearly all the mysteries of the subconscious realm have been brought to light and yet what more have we learned about man's soul than our ancestors knew! For years we have been flying through the air, and now we are shooting pictures through the air. For years we were harnessing waterfalls to turn great turbines, and now we harness the split atoms to fight our battles for us. We are setting in motion powers such as our fore-fathers never dreamed of. But how few of us have learned that the power of prayer is greater than the radio and the power of love greater than the atomic bomb?

Yes, with all our vaunted progress, what has it brought us? The thirty years between 1915 and 1945 have seen more people killed, more property destroyed, more ter-rible cruelty and savagery released in the hearts of man-kind than has occurred in the entire history of the world from the time of Christ until the year 1915. I have made the assertion before audiences in all the largest cities of America that I could have gone into any insane asylum in the country in 1915 and picked out the thirty worst cases and put them at the heads of the thirty greatest governments and let them conduct the affairs of the nations for the following thirty years and the world would not have been any worse off by 1945 than it is now. *And I couldn't find a single person willing to debate it with me.*

Some of us who have taken careful stock of the world as it is today believe that the whole predicament of modern man springs from his limiting his search for solutions to a level too low. The only way to overcome trouble is to come up over it. To extricate ourselves and our world from the dilemma it is in we should "raise our sights." We must set a higher goal and start climbing. The purpose of Part One is to chart a pathway that may help some to make that upward climb.

PART I

"Seek First the Kingdom of Heaven"

CHAPTER I

The Four Known Dimensions of Man

THIS world, we are told, is a world of three dimensions —length, breadth and height. The first dimension consists of a straight line and those who live in that dimension move from one point straight to another point with no digression right or left. The second dimension is at right angles to the first; it spreads out to the right and left in space but is incapable of moving upward or downward. The third dimension is at right angles to the second and spreads above and below. If the first dimension is a line, the second is a square, and the third is a cube.

The normal place of the snail is the realm of one dimension; it always travels on a straight line toward its food. The normal place of the dog is the realm of two dimensions; it moves over a square surface in search of two things—something to eat, and someone to love. The normal place of man is the third dimension; he seeks three things—food and friends and knowledge.

When man is pressed back into one of the lower dimensions there is abnormality of some kind. The man compressed into one dimension is the insane man, completely obsessed with one idea; or he is the thoroughly conditioned criminal whose conscience regarding right and wrong is dead, whose anti-social tendencies have completely blunted all natural affection. He has only one center of reference—self.

The man of two dimensions is one who confines his attention to his gains and appetites and that of his immediate family without any regard to what happens to others.

The man of three dimensions has eyes for his work and his family but also for the higher values of life—education, religion, art, and literature. His chief limitation is that he thinks of himself and his family as entirely separate from all others. Moreover, because he knows that his associates who sink back into the lower dimensions are abnormal, he complacently brands all those who rise to higher dimensions as also abnormal. In other words, he considers anyone who attempts to function outside his own personal status quo as a little bit queer.

If we should take a bird's eye view of the world of three dimensions we should see people, cattle, horses, automobiles and trains—all solid creatures of various shapes and sizes—pinned down to the heavy earth by the law of gravity, moving ponderously about from one place to another through leisurely intervals ticked off on our clock called Time.

But with the marvelous inventions of radar and television we are on the threshold of a new dimension opening to man independent of the laws of gravity.

"If with the aid of sensitive mechanical instruments such as radio, radar and television, we try to picture the world of four dimensions, we would see or hear or feel the atmosphere around us filled with movements, currents and forces entirely independent of gravity, circling, spiralling, and radiating in every possible combination, utilizing every possible wave length—requiring only some sensitive receiving or recording instrument plugged in to the same wave length to reveal their hidden secrets in moving pictures or vibrant sound. If we would use a still more sensitive instrument than radio or television, to wit our enlightened imagination, we could penetrate into the realm of infinitely more thrilling, more powerful forces, currents and movements spiralling and radiating out from trillions of stars, constellations and solar systems—powerful currents that are called cosmic rays spreading out in all directions and re-radiating again from every stellar body they strike. These rays are each one of different mineral and magnetic composition and wherever two intersect a different electrical and chemical reaction is produced. As the rotating planets cut through these rays in their spiralling motion around the sun, all the life upon this globe is produced. Scientists have for some time been trying to tell us that this unseen, vibrating life which is playing through all space is really a tangible, and definite manifestation which, if we only had eyes to see, would appear much more crowded and intricate to our sight than our everyday physical world." *

According to the scientists this earth that seems so heavy and tangible and solid is 57 times more porous than the ether through which it moves. Imagine, if you can, a feather floating through a rock! Incredible as it may seem that is what the earth is like as it floats through the ether. The earth has only one ingredient the ether does not have and that is cohesion. If some unifying principle should start to work in the interstellar spaces where the chemical reactions of the cosmic rays are intermingling and occur-

* The Fifth Dimension and the Future of Mankind! Vera Stanley Alder, Rider & Co., London.

ing, we should see a new and heavier planet suddenly brought to birth.

This, then, is the fourth dimension. It is the plane which gives passage to the electrical and other life forces that are completely independent of gravity. If a man could lift his consciousness to the fourth dimension and always function there he would be able to see and hear in every direction at once to any distance and he would travel through all space with the speed of electricity. Today the improvements in radar, radio and jet planes hint that this time is not so far off.

The man of four dimensions is no longer confined, as the man of three dimensions, to the little spot in space where he happens to stand. Through the magic of radio and radar, through the aid of telephone, telegraph and television and airplane and jet plane hardly a sight or sound upon this earth can escape him. And now with the world-wide acceptance of telepathy it is only a question of time before the thoughts of a man in New York, without mechanical transmitter of any kind, may be able to reach his friend in Los Angeles.

But not only can the man of four dimensions step outside this *space,* but he can also step outside this *time* and see himself in all the moments of the past before Now and in all the moments of the future after Now. This view contrasted with the average man's view is like seeing in a cinema the 26,000 snapshots that pass in sequence before the eye contrasted with a single snapshot projected by the old-fashioned magic lantern. A man who has this fourth dimensional view of his past and future, when brought face to face with a man whose view is confined to his three-dimensional present self, is irresistible. Alexander the Great as a youth slept every night with a copy of

Homer's story of Achilles under his pillow, and Napoleon slept with a copy of the Life of Alexander the Great under his pillow. These men looked into the timeless past for their inspiration, they visioned the years of future victory as already theirs. When Alexander started forth with a small army to conquer the world, an advisor said, "If you go forth to conquer, these are too few; if it be to be conquered, they are too many." To this Alexander replied, "You forget I have my *hopes.*" His hopes were fourth-dimensional, and through his hopes he conquered.

One of my college boys could not walk until he was eleven, but he pasted pictures of famous runners on the walls of his bedroom, and day-dreamed of the time when his own feet would be speeding over the ground. When he was sixteen, he ran the fastest quarter-mile ever run in the high schools in Minnesota. His fourth-dimensional viewpoint made him irresistible.

The fourth-dimensional man is the man who brings the daydreams of his youth to add impact to the present, and who in middle life continues to hold before himself a vision to live for and a purpose to work for, clear up to the very end.

The characteristic of the third-dimensional man is his individuality, his points of difference, his *separateness* from everyone and everything else. With the split-up of the Roman Empire, and the Holy Catholic Church, the *third dimension* simply ran riot in the world for a thousand years. Churches were divided and then sub-divided. Nations broke off from nations. Bacon's "Novum Organum" replaced Aristotle's "Organum," supplanting the old deductive reasoning with the modern inductive reasoning. Molecules were divided into atoms and atoms into electrons until they reached the point where no further

sub-division seemed possible. The key word that dom-
inated the thinking world was *analysis*. The summit of
the three-dimensional outlook was when *everything was
separate from everything else*. There came a time when
all this three-dimensional thinking culminated in two
World Wars. We had reached the paralysis of analysis.

Then began the Age of the Fourth Dimension. An army
of scientists pioneered the way as prospectors, pathfinders
and promoters. The radio, airplane and television began
breaking down the thin walls of partition that kept men
apart and changed the emphasis of the age from *separate*
to *penetrate*. The scholar followed the scientist by changing the key word from *analysis* to *synthesis*. The very air
became so charged with the new rhythm toward Union
that any attempt to disunion resulted in terrible repercus-
sions and catastrophes.

Union and *penetration* are the key words we shall be
hearing in this new age, nor has the old tradition of separateness power to stand before them. As the radio air-
waves carry sound rhythmically from one part of the
world to another, as the airplanes carry people rhythmically from one place to another, so our daydreams and
visions and definite life purposes can carry the freshness
and vigor of one's youth into middle age, and the power
and wisdom of middle age can create permanent accom-
plishments on down through the centuries. All these things
belong to the Fourth Dimensional Era of Living.

Anyone who would explore this new dimension and tap
its possibilities should note carefully that this penetrating,
traveling, conveying power of the fourth dimension,
whether it goes through time or space, is greatly increased if it is done rhythmically and gracefully and joyously rather than jerkily, spasmodically and gloomily.

Put harmony and joy into your radio broadcast through space, and put even more joy and harmony into your day-dream broadcast through time, if you would experience this new dimension at its best.

There was one advantage in living in a three-dimensional world. By holding mankind in bondage to gravity, the confining walls of Time and Space served as a protective sieve to ration the stimulus of the outer world slowly enough for mankind to assimilate it properly. On the other hand, the disadvantage of these confining walls of the third-dimensional world was that it separated each man from everyone else. In that age the slogans heard the most were, "The survival of the fittest," "Everyone for himself," and "The devil take the hindmost." The world became divided into nations, and the nations into classes. Prejudice, bigotry and intolerance ran wild. Man came to adore his physical world and lived only for what it could give him. As the world consisted of solid objects that one could handle and own, greed and covetousness took possession of man. He sought multiplicity rather than simplicity, as revealed in the degeneracy of his architecture into fussiness, his college courses into a hundred different subjects, and his home into a storehouse filled with gadgets.

The fourth-dimensional viewpoint restores the world to unity again. The problem is whether man, posited in this old solid world, can stand the growing pains that all the stimulus of the whole world pouring into him at once brings upon him. We are right now like the man who is halfway across the turbulent stream, wondering whether it would be safer to go on ahead or turn back. Our only hope is to go on ahead, trusting that we will safely reach the solid shore of the fifth dimension.

CHAPTER II

The Mysteries of God's Fifth Dimension

I F EACH dimension is at right angles to the last and if the fourth is a dimension of movement in contrast to the stodgy confinements of the third, we may well expect the fifth dimension to be also more stationary—an anchor, perhaps, for this feverish electric age into which we are just entering.

And that is exactly what we find. When you see a score of carpenters threading in and out of a great structure that they are erecting, you can be positively sure that somewhere there is resting, motionless and unmoving, the complete blue-print of the building. When an apple tree grows, expands, and produces apples, you can know very well that that entire tree reposed for a long time, whole, perfect and complete, within the tiny seed of an apple. When the air is filled with a new piece of music caught up by your radio, you can know that the music is on a sheet of paper somewhere, without a note or word missing, and that while the song is spreading faster than light all over the nation, the singer himself is quietly standing in one place in an inner room, where his family or any of his friends could easily find him.

That is the fifth dimension. It is the reservoir where all the patterns floating through space above the rhythms, vibrations and radiating waves are stored. In contrast to the fourth dimension which was all motion, the fifth dimension is poised, eternally at rest.

Let us pause a while as we contemplate this marvelous area of God's universe. Here we find all the dreams and all the fulfillments of mankind. We have at last reached the Secret Place of the Most High, where neither vibration nor rhythm is the key word. We are now on the verge of a great discovery, the discovery that what all these rhythms and vibrations in this world are doing is to bring into manifestation marvelous riches, lovely treasures, beautiful masterpieces that are already there!

We stand where Moses stood when he heard Jehovah's command, "Build according to the pattern given you in the Mount." Is that the command recognized by all the great ones of this earth? The greatest of all said, "I did not do these works but the Father in me doeth them." Just as the miner does not claim to create the coal that he mines, but merely sinks a shaft to where the coal was made a billion years before he was born, so the great artists and philosophers agree with Robert Browning:

"Truth is within ourselves, it takes no rise
From outward things, whate'er you may believe.
There is an inmost center in us all
Where truth abides in fulness; and around,
Wall upon wall, the gross flesh hems it in,
This perfect, clear perception which is truth.
A baffling and perverting carnal mesh
Binds it, and makes all error; and to know
Rather consists in opening out a way
Whence the imprisoned splendor may escape,
Than in effecting entry for a light
Supposed to be without."

And what was Jesus' secret? He opened a way straight to God and put himself in complete alignment with the Father. The epics of Homer and Virgil were produced

only after their authors had invoked the Muses to produce
the Great Song through them. By this invitation they were
putting themselves in alignment to let the All-Song which
God had already composed sing in cadences that mankind
might hear.

The author of the drama of Job, said by many to be
the greatest work of literature in any language, gave practical testimony that such was exactly the way this masterpiece and all masterpieces of wisdom and beauty are produced. In Chapter 28 he describes in matchless poetry the
way gold and precious stones are discovered by the miners.
He compares this with the manner in which hidden wisdom is discovered by going straight to the heart of God.
This way, he explains, should be kept straight by "eschew-
ing evil," which would pull it off the beam. He says the
other force that holds it straight is "the fear of God."
And by "fear" he meant the sense of awe and wonder that
fastens our gaze upon the object without looking right or
left. If this be true, it is not the rhythm, it is not the
vibration that creates the thing. The thing is already there.

True, all these great works sing to us in beautiful
rhythms. True, the oil and coal dug from the earth run
our machinery with the hum of vibration. But note this:
the rhythms and vibrations of the fourth dimension are
merely the *means* of bringing Reality to us, not the Reality itself. The waves of the sea are mere surface manifestations, the mighty ocean abides beneath, motionless and
changeless and undisturbed.

This all reveals to us that if we can go to the sources
from which these rhythms and vibrations come, we shall
find the perfect patterns—infinite, eternal, motionless,
changeless—the contemplation of which will bring one
into a state of eternal ecstasy, glory and bliss.

"Let us go!" I can hear you exclaim. "Why waste time? That is almost too good to be true. Hurry up and show us the way!"

"Show us the way," is what the disciples demanded of Jesus, and he replied, "I am the Way." Jesus is the perfect Pattern. Put yourself in alignment with him and you will be in alignment with all-truth, all-love, all-life. When one's land is right over an oil field, he doesn't have to ask the direction to the nearest oil station. All he needs do is to sink a shaft *straight* to the supply beneath his feet. Note that word, *straight* (eschew evil and fear God). Where is this Kingdom of bliss and glory? Jesus was asked. "The Kingdom," he replied, "is within you."

"And how do we get there?"

"Enter ye in at the strait gate; for wide is the gate, and broad is the way that leadeth to destruction, and many there be that go in thereat; because strait is the gate, and narrow is the way, which leadeth unto life, and few there be that find it."

"What else must we do?"

Your fieldglass may be directed immediately upon something and yet you cannot see the object on account of the blur. That is because the glass is not in focus. Give it a twist and there you are—your two eyes become single, the blur ceases, and the beautiful reality becomes clear to your vision.

And how hard must we work to remove the blur from our vision and reach our treasure? How hard must we work to find Reality?

"No work at all," said Jesus. After you sink the shaft of your will straight into the will of God and after you get your vision focused upon the face of God, you need only become still and wait. God will do all the rest.

"Just look at the lilies of the field," said Jesus. "They toil not, neither do they spin, and yet I say unto you that even Solomon in all his glory was not arrayed like one of these." "Seek ye first the Kingdom of Heaven, (i.e. the Perfect, God-made Pattern) and all these things shall be added unto you."

But isn't that putting a premium on laziness?

Not at all. Note carefully that the lily does what most people (hundreds of millions of them) never even think of doing. It puts itself in perfect alignment with its source of life. It stands erect with its roots resting down deep in the life-giving loam and its petals open wide to the sunshine and rain. The moment the lily allows someone to build a shed above its petals it had better worry. Look about you at the millions of people in the world with sheds of agnosticism over their heads. Behold the millions of heads covered with hate, or worry, remorse and depression.

Jesus also referred to the birds "of the air"—not birds in cages, or fowls fattened for Sunday dinner—but birds free to fly south in autumn and north in spring with the whole world from which to draw their sustenance, not as work but as play, as joyful expression of their emancipated souls.

Ah, there we erase forever all criticism of Jesus as urging laziness. The energy flowing constantly through the lily that is in alignment with the source of life is as great (if we knew how to release it) as is the energy locked up in uranium. The movement of birds through the air always keeping in alignment with the temperate zone, is so rapid that it puts us lazy-bones on earth to shame. And yet never would anyone accuse the lilies of the field and the birds of the air of doing any "work."

And neither can anyone, who really knows, ever accuse our great geniuses—which is the name we give to men who are in alignment with Nature and with God—of doing any work. "I never did a day's work in my life," said Edison. "It was all play because I put my imagination into it." One wouldn't call Michelangelo, Rodin, or Gutzon Borglum lazy, and yet at different times and in different ways each expressed the belief that all he did was to cut away the stone which didn't belong. The statue was already there.

Let us return for a moment to these patterns. A scientist, Dr. Snow, took ten thousand photographs of snowflakes. He found all were beautiful, all were perfect, and no two had the same design. "Scientists have discovered that certain conditions universally produce a characteristic frost pattern upon a glass windowpane, no matter where the windowpane happens to be. These beautiful forms have existed forever out in invisible space, just waiting for a cool windowpane and a cold day to bring them into visibility. Another remarkable thing is that when the sun is veiled, the patterns take the form of ferns or other forms of primeval vegetation which existed on earth when it was shrouded in thick mists. When the sun shines the frost patterns take the form of roses and other sun-kissed flower-shapes." * These patterns are not exclusive to one land—they appear in all lands. They exist somewhere in the infinite treasuries of God and are instantly available anywhere conditions are in alignment to bring them forth.

The great allegories and myths and fairy stories are also in God's vast treasury, all ready to come forth through anyone who is in alignment with God on the one hand and open to the hearts of little children on the other.

* The Fifth, Dimension and the Future of Mankind: Alder, Rider & Co., London.

The Sleeping Princess, symbolic of the awakening of the soul in man, is a tale known in every land of the globe, not passed across the seas from place to place, as some scholars think, but welling up effortlessly through the hearts of simple folk. And Mother Goose rhymes were born in the hearts of mothers and lovers of children even when the tale had never been heard before.

It is just as absurd to imagine that coal was carried from the Ruhr by human hands to the Pennsylvania coal fields as to insist that this and that fairy story was carried from the Aztecs to the Russians or from the Swiss to the English and so on and on, as research scholars are always trying to tell us.

While the man of the fourth dimension, transcending both time and space, is seeking his perfect fulfillment at life's periphery, the man of the fifth dimension rests secure at the center where all the perfect fulfillments abide through all eternity.

Napoleon and Alexander the Great, with all their daydreams behind them extending from the cradle to the grave, toppled over little generals who thought only of the hour and the minute in which they lived. But Jesus did not limit his daydream pictures of himself to the years that extended from the manger to the cross. He knew himself as existing through all time and eternity, in the dreams of his nation for a Messiah from centuries before, and as a Savior of men for centuries to come. "Before Abraham was I am" and "Lo, I am with you alway, even unto the end of the age" were not mere idle words.

The difference between Alexander the Great and the opposing King of Persia was that Alexander was a fourth-dimensional man and the King was a three-dimensional man, and the difference between Jesus and Pilate was that

Pilate was a three-dimensional man and Jesus was functioning as a *five-dimensional* man. When Alexander stood before the Persian generals, the Persian generals were toppled over like ten-pins, and Alexander emerged the winner for that *time*. When Jesus stood before Pilate, Pilate was toppled over and Jesus emerged the winner for all *eternity*.

Now the key word of each dimension is exactly the opposite to the key word of the last dimension. The straight line characterizes one dimension. The square with lines at perfect right angles to the one-dimensional line characterizes two dimensions. The cube, built at right angles to the square, characterizes the third dimension. The multiplication of these cubes in consecutive moments of time characterizes the fourth dimension, giving the impression (as these cubes go flitting past) of continued movement. So in contrast to the penetrating rhythmic movement of constant *becoming* characteristic of the fourth dimension, we come upon the permanent, *static being,* yes, the perfect seeming motionlessness of the fifth dimension.

The man of the fourth dimension eagerly watches the moving pictures flashing past him, eager and curious and at times concerned at what will come next. But the man of the fifth dimension *knows* that *all* the pictures are safely on the reel and that nothing can be taken from them and nothing can be added to them. The fifth-dimensional man, when he starts carving a statue, knows that the statue is already there, perfect and complete, and all he has to do is merely cut away the parts that don't belong. The relationships of the various dimensions can best be shown by the way a genius produces his masterpiece. The great poet knows, for instance, that the All-Song has been already sung in the fifth dimension and that he needs but put himself in rhythmic alignment with that Song and let the rhythms of the fourth dimension write it through him upon paper for the people in the third dimension to read and enjoy.

Very calm and unhurried are the men of the fifth dimension. They move rarely but every move brings something permanent to pass. They never make a waste motion. Most of the things done in these lesser dimensions have to be done over again. A lifetime of grubbing and saving in the third dimension builds a fortune that goes crashing down in 1929. In the fourth-dimensional realm we witness the dreams of *Mein Kampf* dashed into misery and ruin far worse than anything the world had ever experienced before. Had Hitler stepped into the fifth dimension he would have realized the truth in the refrain:

> "Right forever on the scaffold,
> Wrong forever on the throne,
> Yet that scaffold sways the future
> And behind the dim unknown
> Standeth God within the shadow,
> Keeping watch above His own."

And now we come to the question, can we go beyond the fifth dimension? Let us take one peep into the dim unknown and see what we shall see.

CHAPTER III

The Mysteries of God's Sixth Dimension

WHEN we glimpse into the dim unknown above the fifth dimension we find residing in the heart of the sixth dimension a power which, when unlocked, transcends all the powers of the lower five dimensions combined. It is a power that can even modify and alter the so-called unchangeable Divine Plan of the fifth dimension. It is the power of intense feeling filtered through the highest channels known to men—warm and devoted love and yet unpossessive, unselfish, and if need be, sacrificial. "Greater love hath no man than this, that he lay down his life for his friend." "By this they shall know that ye are my disciples, that ye love one another."

One can go through his plodding work in the third dimension and attain some measure of success, but add love for his work and abounding love for his fellow workers and the success will be doubled and tripled immediately. In the fourth dimension of wireless, radio, and telepathy, messages pass from one to another with lightning rapidity, but add love and the sensitivity and effectiveness both in the broadcasting and receiving ends of the line are greatly increased.

Even the patterns of life which have existed in the fifth dimension from the beginning of time can be changed by the powerful influence of unselfish, sacrificial love. "Prophecies may fail," said Paul, "but love never fails." Add the sixth dimension to the fifth and a feeling of fatalism is instantly replaced by a sense of destiny. That is to say, every element in the Divine Plan is seen in proper relationship. "All things work together for good." Evil fades away. If, for instance, your inner divination should foresee death looming near for you on the road ahead, love can turn it into the rapture of stepping into the Kingdom here and now without all that inconvenience of "laying off the mortal coil." If a man is "fated" to lose himself in a power greater than himself, through Love and Prayer, his Divine Destiny can change his course from losing himself in alcoholic spirits that have plagued him in the past, to losing himself in the Holy Spirit that can redeem his life in the present and future. Jesus possessed this sixth-dimensional love, and behold how he could raise even the dead to life! He said we, too, could have that power through this simple formula: "When two or three agree together asking anything in the sixth dimension (i.e. in his loving name) whatsoever ye ask shall be done."

Let us pause for a moment to contemplate again how infinitely more powerful each higher dimension is than the dimension lower down. The dog is more powerful than the moth and the man is more powerful than the dog. Likewise, the fourth dimension, when understood and applied, releases much greater forces than the third. "An average man would naturally think that a stone hatchet was more powerful than a hatchet made of gas," writes Alder, "but when he sees the way an acetylene blowpipe cuts through metals—even under water, where a hatchet would be hopelessly inadequate, he quickly changes his mind." Whenever fourth-dimensional forces are used, they are able to master anything in the third-dimensional realm.

The fifth-dimensional forces whenever they are brought into play are likewise far more powerful than anything the fourth dimension can offer. Think what tremendous power must be at work to hold a design permanently in the atmosphere immune to any disturbances or conditions whatever! Electricity, which belongs to the fourth dimension, powerful as it is, can be turned on and off at will. But this mysterious fifth dimension is independent of all these laws and conditions. The patterns are there engraved upon the cosmic mountains of the Lord, held permanent in the ethers, sustained by the great primal forces of creation. No force on sea or land can destroy them. Like the fruits of the Spirit described by Saint Paul, "against these there is no law."

Can anything be more powerful than these perfect designs held in permanent place in the fifth dimension? Yes, there is a greater power, the mere fringe of which I have touched upon in this chapter. As the hardest glass can be cut by a diamond, so even our fifth dimensional patterns may be modified and improved and lifted into higher usefulness through the mysterious powers of love.

As each new dimension is at right angles, or in complete contrast, to the one before, and as the fifth dimension is motionless, so we would naturally expect the sixth dimension to be filled with motion. But it must be a higher, more invisible motion than the motions of the fourth dimension. And so we discover it *is* much more powerful than electricity and more revealing than radio. Instead of the radiation of electricity, of wireless, of radio and of television, it is the radiation from the souls of men upon this earth and in heaven.

"The two greatest commandments," said Jesus, "are love the Lord thy God with all thy heart, and with all thy soul, and with all thy mind, and love thy neighbor as thyself." Upon these two commandments hang all the law (of the fourth dimension) and the prophets (of the fifth dimension). And he summed up his ministry in the simple words, "By this shall all men know ye are my disciples in that ye love one another."

Strange, is it not, that the emotion we think we are the best acquainted with, the feelings that are most rooted in and native to our being, are the strongest forces in the universe and we knew it not? At first we resist it—we can't believe it. But don't you remember how Jesus said, "A prophet is not without honor except in his own country"? Love is the "Prophet emotion" in man, abused, discredited, unhonored and unsung. No, I must qualify that. No quality in man has been so often glorified and sung about. But no quality has been so misused, so misunderstood, and in its highest reaches so neglected.

Nevertheless, it is a power infinitely greater than electricity, than the atom bomb, than the hydrogen bomb, than anything discovered or invented by man. And yet, like the Holy Grail that Sir Launfal sought throughout the breadth of the land, it has been waiting all this time right at our palace gate. But is it not true that electricity was also all around us, in our sky and earth and only in the last century discovered and put to use? Is it not true that uranium was always in the earth beneath our feet and only discovered as a source of power within the last decade? Therefore, why should we be surprised to learn that Love, which man has been writing poetry about for a thousand years, and alternately scoffing and extolling, is suddenly discovered to have power enough literally to save the world? And yet it has been lying largely unused within us all the time. Now we know what Jesus meant when he said, "The kingdom of heaven is within you."

Paul of Tarsus, two thousand years ago, summed this up beautifully when he said:

"Though I speak with the tongues of men and of angels and have not Love, I am become as sounding brass or a tinkling cymbal. And though I have the gift of prophecy (of the fifth dimension), and understand all mysteries (of the fourth dimension), and all knowledge (of the third dimension), and have not Love (of the sixth dimension), I am nothing. Love never faileth, but whether there be prophecies (on the fifth dimension) they shall fail; whether there be tongues (on the fourth dimension) they shall cease; whether there be knowledge (on the third dimension) it shall vanish away. For we (on the lower dimensions) know in part, and we prophesy in part. But when that which is perfect is come, then that which is in part shall be done away.

"When I was a child I spake as a child, I understood as a child, I thought as a child; but when I became a man, I put away childish things. For now we see through a glass darkly; but then face to face; now I know in part; but then shall I know even as also I am known.

"Finally there abideth faith (in the fourth dimension), hope (in the fifth dimension), and love (in the sixth dimension); these three; but the greatest of these is love."

CHAPTER IV

The Mysteries of God's Seventh Dimension

WE HAVE been going up a series of stairways, each step taking us a little closer to God. Because these are such important steps, each one carrying the implications, almost, of a rebirth, we have used the definitive word "dimensions" instead of the figurative word "steps." The level or dimension where most of us stop and live and move and have our being is the third—the place where the solid, stuffy people live. The fourth level brings us to the place where the rhythmic, dancing people live. Here the solid matter is melted up into protons and electrons, and all matter is seen as nothing but energy in motion, and the minds of men are engaged in the rhythms of radio, radar, television and telepathy.

Next we stepped into the fifth dimension, where the peaceful people live—in other words, the area above all vibrations and rhythms of the fourth dimension where are to be found the perfect patterns for every person and every nation and every event if we can clear away the fogs sufficiently in our minds and souls to see them. As long as a vessel is ploughing through thick fog banks, its navigators have to keep their radar working constantly to catch the return vibrations from any iceberg or jutting headland that may endanger the journey. But when the mist is all cleared away, no longer does the captain have to depend upon instruments to record vibrations—he can steer the course easily and rhythmically into the harbor that awaits him, because now he can *see* the perfect course before him.

Jesus, who could *see* the perfect pattern of each disciple, cautioned his seventy not to be so thrilled over the vibrations they could control in the fourth dimension by which they could cast out demons, but to rejoice rather that their perfect patterns in the fifth dimension were already created for them in heaven.

The sixth dimension might be called the place of orchestration, where all these patterns, in other words these "names that are written in heaven," can be brought together in perfect agreement and harmony. Jesus defined this dimension when he said, "If two of you shall agree (symphonize) on earth as touching anything that they shall ask, it shall be done for them of my Father which is in heaven."

It was stated when we were considering the fifth dimension, that just *one* person, when he got still enough for the fogs to roll away, and the blur to leave his vision, would be able to see his Divine Plan or the "pattern given in the Mount" so clearly that great things could come through him. The All-Song would then sing through him, or the perfect guidance come to him, or the exact supply for his needs appear when the need called.

But when, not you alone, but two or three others join with you and get just as still, grow just as clear, and see just as vividly, then the Power that comes through will be greatly multiplied. When seven or twelve agree, the power becomes tremendous. When one hundred and twenty come together in one place and all are of one mind, the Event will be heralded in heaven and upon earth as a Pentecost.

In the fifth dimension we found that there is a particular plan for each of us, just as there is a pattern for each snowflake. In the sixth we see many patterns brought into union, symphonized in power and beauty, as an orchestra brings numbers of instruments together to produce something that no instrument playing alone can achieve. Ultimately in the seventh dimension we find *The Pattern* which unites *all* patterns in the heart of God Himself. The great step that the saints have made in more or less degree, but only Jesus has made perfectly, is to abide so completely in the Father that the Father and they are one. "He that hath seen me hath seen the Father; and how sayest thou then, Shew us the Father?"

In Portland, Maine, I once witnessed a *complete* eclipse of the sun. Because the form of the moon is made after the image and likeness of the sun, both being perfect spheres, when the moon swings in its orbit in front of the sun it shuts out the view of the sun entirely. Let us imagine that you are the moon and God is the sun and completely reverse the process—the world would be flooded with light. Whenever man lets God swing in *front* of *him,* letting his little self be completely erased from view by the greater Self of God, something wonderful happens!

One who achieves this is called a mystic. Don't be afraid of that word. Before you decline it, define it! "Mysticism," says Evelyn Underhill, "means *union with Reality.*" And the greatest of all Realities is God! The simplest way to achieve this union is through absolute surrender, through completely losing oneself in the Absolute God. Jesus has himself defined it in many different ways—all of them more beautiful than any dictionary definition could be. The one I like best is, "He who would lose his life shall save it." Another is, "I am the Vine; ye are the branches." And in his prayer in the Upper Room Jesus ended with a special intercession for you and for me. When he finished praying for his disciples he said, "Neither pray I for these alone, but for them also which shall believe on me through their word; that they all may be one; as thou, Father, art in me, and I in thee, that *they also may be one in us."*

As we are branches and Christ is the Vine, the biggest decision that we must make in life is where we shall take our stand; shall we let our consciousness—our awareness —rest where the branch connects with the Vine, or out at the tip far away from the center, exposed to every wind of emotion and desire that blows?

That is the battle that Job had to fight when his great calamity fell upon him. In the presence of his very conservative friends he was faced with the dilemma—should he declare himself as united with God or with the dust of the earth? At which end of the branch should he take his stand? Should he be modest and tell a falsehood; or should he be true and appear to others to be boastful and arrogant? He listened deep down in his heart, and there he found only one answer. "Be true to the highest light you have; there is no other way. Speak the truth as you see it and know it, even though the heavens fall."

And what was it that down in his heart he knew? Simply this, that in his essential nature, in his real self, the self which is of God, and through which God speaks, acts and thinks, he *was* perfect. He knew that the utterance of these words would in themselves condemn him in the eyes and before the traditions of those who sat with him. Therefore he said, "If I speak, my own words will condemn me." Nevertheless he exclaimed, "I am perfect; I regard not myself!"

Notice that he did not say, "I declare *myself* to be perfect," but "I AM perfect." In this inner struggle there was evidence that the author of Job made a distinction between the I which is subjective, within, governing, controlling, creating; and the *me* which is objective, without, governed, controlled, created. There is a distinction between the creator and the creation. Man as the creator is perfect, one with God; man the creation is imperfect, one with the earth.

Everywhere in the Bible humility is counselled, and usually as the very highest good. But it is always humility and humiliation of the outer, objectified *me;* never of the creative and life-building *I.*

The publican's prayer is commended to us by Jesus, but it is noteworthy that he did not say, "I AM a sinner, be merciful to me," but "God, be merciful unto *me, a* sinner." When the young man came worshipping Jesus, Jesus did not say, "I AM not good" or "I AM not worthy to be called good." What he did say was, "Why callest thou *me* good? Only one is good, the Father which is in heaven." His spiritual intuition told him that the young man was not worshipping the inner Heavenly Father, the divine *I* in Jesus, but the outer personality of the human *me,* and he would have nothing to do with it.

The final test of spiritual insight, spiritual discernment, spiritual understanding, is the power of one to see in another not the *me* but the I. Great spiritual natures who have fastened themselves to the Father or, rather, who see and recognize their union with the Father, make that the test of finding the spiritual union with others.

God made one definition of Himself, the only time He

ever defined Himself according to the Bible: "I AM that I AM." Someone has said that we take God's name in vain whenever we say, "I AM sick, I AM wicked, I AM hopeless," etc. We can say, "Sickness has come to *me*" or "Sin has fallen upon *me*" or "Despair has come upon *me*" if we wish. What is the difference, one may ask? There is a whole world of difference. The "I" way of talking assumes that sickness, sin and despair are parts of ourselves, integrally related to us, permeating us, staining and saturating us. It is this philosophy of taking the name of the Lord in vain that has led men to believe that the way to get rid of sin was to destroy and punish the sinner; that when a man was sick it was in some cases impossible to cure him; that when a man was in despair he had something to despair of.

But when we think of these things as falling upon, or attacking the objective me from the outside, not the inner I part of ourselves, we see that sin, sickness and unhappiness are merely like dead leaves falling upon our hat brims, or like records played upon a phonograph—something which may be easily brushed away or *lifted off,* leaving the hat unstained and the victrola ready to receive a new and better record.

Job said, "I AM perfect; I regard not *myself,*" thus hinting that he took his stand with the I part of his nature and not the *me* part. Because he thus classed himself as an equal and co-equal with God rather than with the worms, he was reviled by his friends and accounted as the greatest sinner of his time. When Jesus said, "The Father and I (not *me*) are one," he gave the chief weapon the Pharisees needed to condemn him. However, God put his stamp of approval upon these statements of Job when he spoke out of the whirlwind and said, "Job had spake wisdom unto his friends"; and when he spoke out of the sky to Jesus, "This is my beloved Son, in whom I am well pleased." But in spite of all this, the *good* men of Job's day condemned Job, and the *good* men of Jesus' day crucified Jesus. "For what good work do you condemn me?" asked Jesus of the Pharisees. "For no good work," they replied, "but because, being a man, you make yourself equal to God."

And today? Whenever one takes his stand with the I within him which is united with God—then miracles begin to occur around him because he lives, moves, and has his being in the creative, God-like part of his nature instead of in the created, manifested, material side of his nature. People will then willingly accept the miracles, wonder at them, celebrate them, and advertise them, and even exploit them, but they may turn upon him, and condemn him, call him queer and fanatical, and advise the orthodox to stay away. And yet has not Jesus said, "Greater works shall ye do, because I go to the Father"? We can hear him say, "The Father and I are one; I am perfect; I am the Alpha and the Omega; I am the power to create; I am the power to conceive and express truth; I am the power to love. Before Abraham—(the outer, objectified, physical Abraham)—I AM."

And is it not true that the I, the power to create which resides within us all, existed before any created thing existed? How could a creation exist before the power to create existed? And the power to create that is in you and in me must be of the same essence as the power to create that is in God—part of that great, eternal, All-in-All which works through, in and over all of us. Before the physical manifestation of Abraham existed, the Christ power to create that outer expression of man surely existed, that power that is a part of you as well as of me, as surely as it is of God. Does that make us seem too much like gods? What did Jesus say, when the Pharisees chided him upon calling himself the Son of God? "Did not the Scriptures say, Ye are gods?" and then he added, "And the Scriptures cannot be broken."

Yes, we can take our stand at the inner end of the branch that connects us with the Vine, instead of residing out at the tip of the branch. We can be one with the Great I AM THAT I AM; we can be more than mere manifestations, for we are manifestors as well. Through us God does His manifesting, all of it, if we but knew the ultimate mystery of creation. For when we are in tune with God, our will one with his will, our mind one with his mind, all our desires and wishes and thoughts and plans can come into manifestation.

For we are then creators, co-workers with the great I AM.

CHAPTER V

A Survey of All the Dimensions

NOW THAT we have reached the seventh dimension, let us pause and take a bird's eye view of the dimensions through which we have travelled.

As we look back upon the first dimension we see it was a mere line, the second a plane, and the third a cube. Mankind living in the third dimension conceived of himself as weighed down by gravity and *separated* from everyone else. In contrast to that, the fourth dimension becomes revealed as a place of *motion,* everything penetrating everything else. The fifth dimension makes another right angle turn, and in contrast to this fourth dimension of *motion,* is revealed as a dimension of *motionlessness.* Therefore when we reach the sixth dimension we expect to *move again,* but this time we discover that the motion is on a grander, more celestial scale than the motion of the fourth dimension, for its root lies not in the telepathy of thought but in the telepathy of love. The *motionlessness* of the fifth dimension proves to be the perfect pattern at the end of the rainbow which was dimly glimpsed by the fourth-dimensional man. The new sixth-dimensional motion does not add anything further to the individual's separate pattern of life, but it brings a perfect interweaving of his pattern with all the other patterns of mankind, beginning with the "mutuals" that God has especially given him. When two or three can agree together, bringing Christ right into their midst, the bliss of the sixth dimension is experienced. And so we discover that the key word of the sixth dimension is *orchestration.*

And this leads to the culmination toward which all these dimensions are moving, and brings into clear light the key word that marks the seventh, the crux and crown of all our earthly and heavenly endeavor—*Oneness.* By this is meant the universal oneness with one's neighbor, oneness with God the Father, oneness with Christ. The motionlessness of the seventh dimension at its very highest is expressed in the greatest of all the parables of Jesus, the parable of the Vine and its branches.

Jesus' teachings, when properly understood, constitute the only authentic road-map for reaching the sixth and seventh dimensions. Nevertheless, he himself, being the perfect union of humanity and divinity, had dominion over *all* the dimensions. "I have many things that I cannot tell you now." Gradually, whenever and wherever he could, he introduced his people to a new dimension, one step at a time, each above where they had been last. But he cautioned his disciples not to travel too fast. "Cast not your pearls before swine, neither give that which is holy unto the dogs, lest they trample them under foot and turn and rend you."

But someday, he prophesied, there will be enough of you living, moving and having your being in the fifth, sixth and seventh dimensions, and when that time comes, "greater things than I have done ye shall then be able to do."

He spoke of the fourth dimension when he said, "When thou prayest, enter into thy closet, and when thou hast shut the door, pray to thy Father which is in secret; and thy Father which seeth in secret shall reward thee openly."

Of the fifth dimension when he said, "Your names are written in Heaven."

Of the sixth dimension when he said, "If two of you shall agree on earth as touching anything that they shall ask, it shall be done for them of my Father which is in Heaven."

Of the seventh dimension when he said, "I pray that they may be one, even as we are one: I in them and thou in me, that they may be made perfect in one." Yes, that is the culmination—"that all may be perfect in one." "At that day ye shall know that I am in the Father, ye in me and I in you."

In these four statements you can read the key words of the four highest dimensions: penetration, motionlessness, orchestration and oneness.

When one enters a new field of thought he has to learn a new language. Experts in child psychology don't apologize for the repetitions of words in the primers they put into children's hands. As Part One of this book is a primer in the higher dimensions and as a thorough understanding of these dimensions will make all the subsequent sections clear, I know my readers will forgive me if before we leave this section I make a rapid review of the ground we have covered, restating the fundamental principles in slightly different terms and from a fresh viewpoint. So with this end in mind let us go back again to the very roots of things.

In the first place, we learned that the world of the snail and the moth is not our world. These creatures are one-dimensional; they move in a straight line. They are repelled or attracted by each stimulus presented to them, otherwise they do not see it or cognize it at all. They live in a world governed entirely by sensation. They have no power of grouping many sensations into a perception. If they could, they would graduate from their world into a two-dimensional world.

In the second place, we learned that the dog and the cat live in a world which is not our world. True, they have the capacity of grouping many sensations together to make a perception, but they have not the power of grouping these perceptions to make a conception. They can, for instance, group the sensation of pain which dashing into an attractive yellow flame inflicts upon them, with other similar sensations, and come to a distinct perception that flames should not be dashed into, something the moth can never understand. So while the moth is destroyed in the flame, the dog can change its course, i.e. step out of the straight line into a line at right angles to the destructive object, and go around it. Thus the dog is two-dimensional, has width as well as length to his world. But the sky remains one plane to him, and because he cannot get a "conception" of anything but merely a perception, the building he passes each morning is a new building every day, just as the sunrise each day seems to us to be a new day, and the spring a new spring.

Now if you notice carefully, you will see that each step into a higher conception brings to us a greater power of *unifying the experience of our lives on a lower dimension.* The being who possesses sensation only, lives in one dimension; the being which can unify these sensations into perceptions lives in two dimensions; the being which can unify perceptions into conceptions lives in three dimensions. Man enters here.

But until man can unify his individual, personal conceptions into universal conceptions, he does not become a four- or five-dimensional creature. Consequently he lives in a world of time instead of Eternity. As the one-dimensional thought-world of the moth and snail is cancelled out by the higher-dimensional thinking of the dog, and as the thinking of the dog is cancelled out by the higher thinking of man, in the same way we may know that most of our thinking about life and our efforts to formulate a philosophy of life will be false and so much effort wasted if they proceed on a three-dimensional scale of selfishness, prejudice, hate and fear, instead of on a still higher dimensional scale of unselfishness, faith and love. And how can we reach that higher scale? The first requirement is to leap the chasm of separateness and *see unity in all things.* We must accept our dwelling place not as a multiverse but as a universe. The boundaries of time conceal that unity from three-dimensional creatures, just as the boundaries of space conceptions prevented the lower creatures from seeing unity in sensations or unity in perceptions.

Our initial purpose, then, should be to see unity in the Universe. Once get this *realization* clear, and you have taken your first stand in higher thinking, and all the truths of life will become increasingly clearer to you as you proceed.

A mosquito, for instance, bites a man's foot and then his hand, but is not aware that these limbs are parts of the same man. A dog sees his master as a whole man and is faithful to *him,* but he does not understand that the stranger who rushes into his master's arms is his long-lost brother.

And now comes the three-dimensional man, who recognizes the two men as brothers, members of the same family, but does not recognize the Japanese or the German whom this man may be fighting as being also his brother, nor does he see that the man he is trying to crush in business is his brother as well. Jesus, when he said, "I am the vine and ye are the branches," when he said, "Ye are my brothers, my sisters and my mother," when he told the parable of the Good Samaritan, lifted mankind with him to the level of higher-dimensional thinking.

As soon as we rise to this *higher realization,* as soon as we attain this *perfect union with reality,* we find that heaven commences to be seen around us. Then complete happiness is ours, correct thinking is ours, perfect friendships are ours, harmonious love, beauty and self-expression are ours. We have become unresisting witnesses to God's imperishable glory. We find also that hell, as far as we are concerned, ceases to exist.

Indeed, what is hell? Hell is merely the confining of our souls in cramping bondage to a lower dimensional world than the one for which we were created. What was the most terrifying nightmare of your childhood? Was it not finding yourself cramped in a drain pipe, or under a porch, so tightly caught you could not get out? Such is the hell many of us confine ourselves in now—the bondage to hypocrisy, hate and fear in a three-dimensional world which we are supposed to outgrow.

How can we escape from hell? By turning to the world of reality above us—turning to God. We escape from evil just as an automobile driver escapes from a signpost in the middle of the road ahead—*he turns.*

Let us trace this further and see where it leads.

The moth, living in a world of mere sensation, governed by his attractions and repulsions and nothing else, is drawn into the flame. Because he cannot unify his sensations so as to create a perception of danger, he does not escape. If he could only turn to the world of reality right beside him, the two-dimensional world of perception of the dog and cat, he could escape as they do, by turning aside. But he cannot and he is therefore destroyed. To the moth, the flame which first represents desire, finally becomes hell.

Now witness a dog cast upon an island of rock and sand. He will soon perish from hunger unless he can contrive snares for birds or nets for fish. By so doing he could *turn from* his world of mere perceptions to a world of conceptions. This he cannot do, hence he dies the lingering death of starvation. Starvation is hell for the dog.

Now witness man engaged in a great world war. Fifty million men, women and children are being butchered like cattle, a hundred million are being dragged into terrible suffering and privation. *Hate is hell, fear is hell, man's failure to see the unity of mankind is hell.*

We make our own hell. Can we unmake it? Certainly. *All we have to do is to turn to the world of reality just above us, the world of higher dimensions, the world where men are all brothers, where they are all branches of the same vine, where all is one vast unity.*

Then we shall see that we cannot hurt our neighbor without also hurting ourselves.

Just as the only escape for the moth from the flame is to turn, the only salvation ahead for man is to turn to an entirely different concept of mankind. All other schemes on a mundane plane are merely different ways of dashing himself into the flame. HE MUST TURN.

I know just how difficult it is for the average reader to form a conception of this higher dimension. It is because each higher plane must be at *right angles* to the plane below, which means that every word that is competent to describe it seems to contradict every word that described the previous plane.

We saw, for instance, how each dimension swallowed up and cancelled out the dimension which preceded it— the line being swallowed in the plane, and the plane in the cube. That brought us to the question, what can be at right angles to the cube, a good, strong, material, physical cube? What is antithetical—opposite—at right angles, so to speak, to material things? Is it not spiritual things? Saint Paul did a good job of contrasting the carnal and the spiritual, showing how the spiritual world swallows up, cancels out, the fragile limitations of the material world. This, then, is the higher-dimensional world, the world of reality toward which we are striving. And because this new world is so exactly opposite to the self-centered world in which most of us live, Jesus never spoke of it except in paradoxes.

As all philosophies of life built upon the single sensation plane of the one-dimensional snail fail, and must be supplanted by the perception plane of the dog and the cat; as the latter must be thrown overboard as so much worthless rubbish when confronted by the three-dimensional philosophy of life in a material world of the philosopher and scientist; even more so, because with each increase in altitude the leap between the "planes" becomes greater, we must throw into the discard as so much sound and foam, as so much chaff and litter, our worn-out philosophy of life geared only to a material universe, and supplant it with *a philosophy of life adapted to and adequate for a spiritual universe.*

Such a philosophy cannot come from ourselves, it must

come from above. But as the material scientists may erect radio wires to catch the thoughts that are passing through the material world, so we may erect altars to catch the celestial thoughts that will come down to us from the spiritual world. That these thoughts may be different for each one of us is, of course, expected. That no two persons may see the same light, or catch the same heat from the same fire, is also to be expected. It is not in the hope of teaching anything new that this is being written, but rather to emphasize the world-shaking truths that Jesus proclaimed and so few of his followers seem able to comprehend. When you step from this mundane level of thinking into the higher dimensions that Christ charted for you you will seem to be in a new world. In this new world you will discover seven things:

I. The first thing that you will discover is that while everything in this world seems to be new, there has been actually no change at all in God's universe, the change has been entirely within *you*. This perfect, harmonious universe was all about you from the beginning of time, merely awaiting your capacity to see it for it to grow within you.

II. The second discovery that will come to you is that each plane is perpendicular to the plane below. Width is perpendicular to length and height is perpendicular to width; time is perpendicular to space and eternity is perpendicular to time, love is perpendicular to hate and peace is perpendicular to war. In other words, each plane is at right angles and in direct antithesis to the other planes below, swallowing them up or cancelling them out in every instance. This means that to enter each new plane you must (and this requires effort) die to the lower world and be born again in the higher; in other words, make a complete *turn*.

III. Third you will discover that after rising into the new plane you see the lower planes spread out before you in their proper perspective, which enables you to see relationships and connections between various parts that you never saw before. That is to say, you see *unity and harmony* where before you saw only *diversity and discord*.

IV. The fourth thing you learn is that after all these changes have occurred within yourself, their effect is the same as if they had created an entirely new world outside of you. That is to say, the new combinations and newly discovered unities of the old, lower dimensions in their new relations to the higher world in which you are moving, bring to pass the sensation of finding the world all over again as an entirely new world, which is a perfectly natural experience for one who is *born again.*

V. The fifth thing you will learn is that what is spoken in secret will be proclaimed from the housetop. A characteristic of the man who lives, moves and has his being in the higher dimensions is that he leads a singularly open life, his thoughts are as clean as his words, for he knows that what one thinks in his heart is manifest in action, what is done in secret becomes visible to the entire world.

VI. The sixth thing you will learn is that evil has no power in itself except the power that you give it. A man who lives in the upper dimensions is characterized by a singular disregard or non-resistance or non-recognition of evil, for he knows it as something that is cancelled out by the incoming current of the vaster, larger life.

In fact he finds that evil is usually something good in the wrong place. A spade-full of rich garden loam is a wonderful thing when dumped in the garden, but a heinous crime when dumped on a banquet table. Thrift is a virtue when used to *guard* the depositor's money, but becomes a vice when expressed in the greed that *steals* it. Love is the greatest of virtues when it feeds others, but becomes lust when it feeds upon others. Covetousness, lust, jealousy, greed, hate and prejudice are cast out of one's life and left far behind us as one makes the turn and rises to a higher dimension where he finds it impossible to do anything else but love God with all his mind, strength, heart and soul, and his neighbor as himself. The upper-dimensional man knows how it is that upon these two Commandments hang all the law and the prophets.

VII. The seventh thing you learn is that to save your life you must lose it. The most outstanding trait of a higher-dimensional man is his *selflessness*. This is a positive, not negative characteristic, as is so commonly supposed. It is a losing of the lower-dimensional life, true—but with perfect knowledge that the greater unity that takes its place leads to an infinitely larger life—he that loseth his life shall truly find it.

Let us imagine a little "practical" moth scolding an idealistic moth who thinks of leaving the life of exquisite, separate sensation for a life where the sensations will be lost—merged in perceptions. "How silly, how foolish, how visionary you are" he tells him. But behold, even while he is chiding, the visionary moth "makes the turn" and escapes the flame of hell in which the other perishes.

And so the practical, prehistoric apeman, munching his bones, smelling the interesting new trails (the same old one is new each day to him), roundly gives a piece of his mind to the dreamer man who thinks he will *turn* and lose his perceptions in concepts, and dreams and plans. But the latter begins to use words and build bridges while the apeman perishes in the flood.

Today this thinking, practical man who uses words and

builds bridges has, alas, been starting wars and inventing unspeakable means of destruction. He laughs to scorn the idealist who says we are all brothers, that nations should make gifts to other nations of food and machinery, that we should break down barriers and destroy our armaments, and substitute love for hate and prayer for argument. "Such outrageous foolishness!" he exclaims.

But—mark my words—we have reached the flame. Millions of our race have already perished. Those who scoff and spread hate will perish, as those who love and build schools will survive. There is no longer time for laughing or scornful words. God is on our right hand. *We must make the turn.*

FOREWORD TO PART II

In Part I we examined the stairways by which man, born as a son of earth, may climb into sonship with God. Union with Earth on the one hand and union with God on the other might pose a hopeless paradox were it not that God sent His Son into this world to show us the way the human and divine may be blended in perfectly adjusted and harmonious relationship when one is in perfect alignment with his God and in perfect rhythm with his fellow men.

In Part II we shall undertake to show how this perfect alignment and perfect rhythm may be attained. Once attained man stands revealed as a unique organism wonderfully and fearfully made as a selective channel to take the coarse, outer substance all around him and filter it upward into higher realms of the Spirit, in a sort of inward breath; and then in an outward breath send it forth again into outer actions, creations and tangible forms of one kind and another. The inward, upward process of turning solids into spirit is called *transmutation*. The breathing forth of the unseen into the seen is called *crystallization*. Man was created by God as a sort of superconscious lung by which this process can be continued indefinitely.

It is a fascinating study to trace the unique way man serves as a catalyst for transmitting the heavy, earthy world into the higher realm of the spirit. The plant through its "lungs" and "digestive apparatus," in other words, through its leaves and roots, takes the carbon and other mineral elements from the earth, transmuting rocks and mud into sugars and salts of cellular life. Man consumes the plant, or, if the cow consumes the plant, man consumes the cow, and thus lifts the salts and sugars and vitamins which originated in the rocks and mud, and converts them all into energy. He uses this energy to create schools and churches and books and philosophical systems. In these philosophical systems and in these churches he finds great basic laws and principles underlying all of life which point to only one thing, a Universal God who creates and controls all of life.

Thus his thinking is transmuted into something still higher: love and gratitude and faith. Through that faith, if it is great enough, he places himself completely and utterly in union with God, until he and God become one.

It is equally fascinating to trace crystallization, the reverse process, by which man also serves as a catalyst in this eternal rhythm of God for stepping this intangible, imponderable, inner experience down into outer manifestation in the practical, every-day life of mankind.

Thus we see that life is a constant poem, a steady, constant rhythm from a higher frequency rate into a lower frequency rate, bringing that which is invisible into visibility; or, conversely, transmuting earthy things from a lower vibration to a higher rhythm, changing something visible to something invisible. Jesus commanded us to fulfill the law of transmutation when he gave the order, "Seek first the Kingdom of Heaven"; and he commanded us to fulfill the law of crystallization when he ordered us to pray "Thy Kingdom come on earth as it is in Heaven."

When we examine this crystallization process we discover that the whole world is but an externalization of man. Just as man as a physical creation is himself merely an expression of the outer world, so is the outer world a picturization of the inner man. We might say that man has absorbed the outer world, drawing from its minerals to form his bones, drawing from the vegetable world to form the cells of his body, drawing from the animals to form his flesh—and *then,* having let the outer world pass through him, as through a filter, so to speak, and working upon it with his mind as a catalyst as it passes through, the outer world comes forth again as elements of a new and higher civilization. Thus we see that man has within himself the expression of everything, great and small, that resides in the universe.

Next we see how, through the marvellous working of his subconscious, inventive capacity, man has externalized, one by one, into objectivity, all the things embraced within himself. "He has externalized his animal propensities in the form of animal deities," writes Vera Stanley Alder. "He has expressed his emotional and imaginative make-up in picture, in tapestry and in poem. He has externalized every muscle and sinew in his body in the form of tools, machines and engines. He has externalized his eyesight in the form of camera and cinema, his hearing in the form of music, telephone and wireless. At present he is endeavoring to capture in externalized instruments the very cosmic ray forces which play through him. His achievements are incessant, untiring and astonishing." *

If a man can externalize his emotions and imagination, his muscles and sinews, and even his sight and hearing, why cannot he externalize those deeper qualities of his soul and character and make of this external world a

* The Fifth Dimension and the Future of Mankind: Rider & Company, London.

veritable Kingdom of Heaven on earth? Why cannot he externalize the thoughts of his mind and the desires of his heart? Jesus said that we could. That was the core and center of His entire message.

There is no doubt that we can externalize our own inner peace of mind upon the outer world provided that we *have* peace of mind. If there are enough of us to try the venture, there is nothing to prevent the love and harmony in our hearts from externalizing itself in the United Nations Council. A hundred cannot do it, neither can a thousand. How many million will it take?

PART II

The Pattern on the Mount

CHAPTER VI

The Law of Alignment

I HAVE found that the whole Art of Living is bound up in the proper understanding and proper application of this magic word, alignment. When one is in perfect alignment with God and man all work becomes play, and all creative effort becomes effortless. An aligned person is an irresistible person.

Jesus gives the secret of alignment in the last verses of Chapter Two in Luke's Gospel. When he was in Nazareth with His parents, he was "subject unto them." But in another verse in the same chapter we find that when Jesus was in Jerusalem passing by the temple he left the caravan of His family and entered the sanctuary where "he was about his Father's business."

Alignment, then, means the putting of that which is higher, high, and that which is lower, low. As a child Jesus placed himself beneath his parents, but in Jerusalem he placed his family below the Temple. Later when he found the Pharisees and the other keepers of the Temple trying to turn religion upside down, putting the *outer* and *lesser* above the *inner* and *greater,* he put the Kingdom of Heaven and its righteousness above the Temple. In His sermon on the Mount he gave a new, clear statement of the Art of Alignment in saying, "When ye pray stand not on corners as the hypocrites do, but enter into thy closet and close the door." It is not what you *do openly* but what you *think inwardly* that counts. And as the climax of the Sermon he sums up all the laws of alignment in one simple sentence, "Seek ye first the Kingdom of God and its righteousness and all these things shall be added unto you."

Let us apply the law of alignment first to the practical, three-dimensional plane where most people live. The efficient life on this three-dimensional plane consists of eliminating waste motions and putting everything of lesser value in subordination to that which is of higher value. In the mechanical world, for instance, it consists of getting the piping as direct from the source to the user as possible, bringing water down from the hills and gas up from the ground without undue waste of time.

The efficient man is the one who walks in rhythm with the laws of the universe and not in opposition to them. Records are constantly being broken on the athletic field as new ways are discovered of eliminating waste motions and releasing one's efforts in more perfect alignment with the native powers within the body. Men can carry great loads up steep mountain paths if they place them correctly upon their shoulders; native women in Africa carry unbelievable weight upon their heads, having mastered the art of keeping all in alignment with a balanced spine.

In the industrial world we find stream-lined automobiles, stream-lined trains, diesel engines, chain stores. Efficiency experts are paid high fees to discover ways of eliminating waste motions among employees, and increasing the output of goods.

In the field of government, efficiency is undoubtedly increased by proper use of what might be called the hierarchy system. The original plan of the founders of this nation was for it to be a republic first and a democracy second. To this end it was planned for the common people not to choose the president, but for some superior men called Electors to do so. These were to constitute the Electoral College to select, out of their superior wisdom, the proper man to govern this great nation. The Christian Science Church, the Mormon Church, the Roman Catholic Church all function through hierarchies and when the right man or group is at the head of things there is no doubt whatever that there is greater efficiency and less waste motion than in the more democratic Protestant churches. Whenever war breaks out a democracy is converted into a dictatorship overnight, as at such times every delay through waste motions might prove fatal. One of the greatest disgraces of our government, due to misuse of our democratic system, is the terrible waste in conducting our nation's business. Overlapping bureaus, red tape, duplication of service, lead to the unnecessary waste of an estimated five billion dollars annually.

The most effective way to get efficiency into the practical activities of this world is to lift our vision into the higher dimensions. One who depends entirely upon his three-dimensional brain to solve all the intricate problems of this world is like the man who tries to lift himself over a fence by pulling on his own boot-straps. To improve the quality of a business output requires first of all improving the quality of the men who participate in it.

Arthur Brisbane in an editorial that reached twelve million readers said, "Big companies are willing to pay fifty thousand dollars a year for men who can sit in office chairs before empty desks and look out the window for four hours a day and think straight; and they can't find

enough men to fill these chairs." In other words, the greatest institutions are seeking men who can put themselves in
alignment with the powers of the universe.

Wherever there is a church properly wired for electricity no effort is required to bring light into the building,
no labor in cleaning lamps, or filling them with kerosene;
the mere touch of a switch will flood the church with
light. Likewise, where there is a church properly aligned
spiritually, no effort is required to bring the Light of
Christ to the congregation. Where the minister is completely and utterly surrendered to God, and where those
next to him—the elders, deacons, trustees, superintendent
of Sunday School and Religious Education Directors—
are only slightly less consecrated than the minister himself, there is no need of putting on church suppers or
bazaars or advertising in the paper to draw crowds. There
is hardly need to preach sermons. Merely to enter a church
where there is such perfect alignment, where First Things
are really put first, where there is such complete, utter
trust in God and such perfect love and mutual trust among
all the members, is like stepping into heaven. Such an
atmosphere of harmony is sufficient to light the flame of
God in everyone's heart.

Where a business firm has such accord among directors,
managers and workers, where a football team has such
harmony among its members, success is assured before the
season starts. Effortlessly, joyously, victory comes.

But how does one achieve such perfect alignment? The
place to begin is within one's own soul, through prayer,
meditation, and forgetting self in the service of others.

Here is a prayer that held a great Saint, Thomas
à Kempis, in constant alignment:

"O Lord, Thou knowest what is the better way, let this or that be done as Thou shalt please. Give what Thou wilt. . . . Deal with me as Thou knowest and best pleaseth Thee, and is most for Thy honor. Set me where Thou wilt, and deal with me in all things as Thou wilt. I am in Thy hand; turn me round and turn me back again, even as a wheel. Behold I am Thy servant, prepared for all things; for I desire not to live unto myself but unto Thee; and oh that I could do it worthily and perfectly!"

If this alignment is perfectly experienced you will find that from that time onward God is everywhere. You will realize that He is present in *all your life,* the *outer* as well as the inner. You will become aware that He is radiating from your face and speaking through your lips and creating beautiful things through your finger-tips. You will experience the exquisite bliss of His love manifesting in your work, bringing harmony among your friends, and new joy into your play.

But greatest of all, when you have come into alignment with God in *all your being* you will be better able to pray for perfect and heavenly alignment to come into your friends, your church, your working associates, and you will be able to pray with new power for the Prince of Peace to become the Lord of Nations, bringing Peace on Earth and good will to men.

CHAPTER VII

The Law of Rhythm

As YOU get quiet on a summer day and become aware of the ripple of the brook, the song of the birds, the ebb and flow of the tides, the beating of the heart, the inspiration and expiration of the breath, the waxing and waning of the moon, the alternation of day and night, the coming and going of the seasons, you begin to realize that God must have created this world as a poet creates a poem, while "the morning stars sang together and all the sons of God shouted for joy." You begin to believe that the ancients were right in their theory of the "Music of the Spheres." They believed that the stars as they moved through the sky created a beautiful symphony, the music of which was so constant that we were not conscious of it, but that if for some reason it should ever cease we should become aware that something very beautiful and precious had dropped out of our lives.

And so we discover that the second great law for bringing the harmonies of heaven into the world around us is the Law of Rhythm.

The scientists have done the spade work in proving to us that the entire material world consists of nothing more or less than rhythms and vibrations.

Dr. Donald H. Andrews, physicist of Johns Hopkins

University said at Stony Run Quaker Meeting House, May 17, 1950, "If there were an atom squeezer which could squeeze atoms together so that only solid material remains, a man could be squeezed down to the size of a very tiny dust speck, and all men now living could be put into a bottle that one could easily carry in one's pocket. All atoms," continued Dr. Andrews, "give off music—vibrations that are rather like light. Each of us is giving off vibrations all the time, something like super-symphonic radiations. Most of these vibrations are in the infra-red range and cannot be seen with the naked eye. In short, we are living in a universe which is built on musical terms rather than materialistic terms. The discovery of atomic music has forced us to a new view."

And that new view is that if we can bring ourselves into rhythm with the Music of the Spheres and ourselves in alignment with the Love of God, which is the foundation for that music, our lives might become masterpieces.

The scientist in his laboratory is not studying matter; he is studying vibrations. In one class he investigates the vibrations of electricity, in another the vibrations of heat, in another the vibrations of light, and in another the vibrations of sound. Everything solid he finds melts into music. "There are definite musical chords," said Dr. Andrews, "which are associated with the various chemicals of the body (and of everything else) and they are giving off their note all the time. The energy in the physical makeup of a single man could supply more power than all the power stations of the world for several months if it could be released under control."

While the scientists in their laboratories are trying to master vibrations, the poet and the painter and the musician in their studies are trying to master rhythms.

All one need do to become an educated man is to understand the mystery of vibration on the one hand, and the mystery of rhythm on the other. Now vibrations, which are most commonly associated with matter, and rhythms, which are most commonly associated with art, belong to the same family. One is the Martha and the other is the Mary of life. All the higher forms of life manifest as rhythm, all the humbler forms of life manifest as vibrations. Rhythm commands, beautifies, creates; vibration serves in the more mundane phases as the hewer of wood and the drawer of water.

Every building and every bridge has some note that it vibrates to, and if a thousand violins stationed in different parts of that structure should play that note long enough the structure would fall. That is why an army crossing a bridge is required to break step. Our military leaders have apparently never forgotten the way an army once marched around Jericho for seven days keeping step and on the seventh day all the trumpets sounded one great note and the walls came tumbling down.

Link, author of *Return to Religion,* was a chain smoker. There was a beautiful rhythm in the way he took a cigarette from his pocket, tapped it, sprung his lighter on it, and sent the smoke curling from his lips. Wishing to break himself of the habit he changed the beautiful rhythm into ugly vibrations. By putting his packet of cigarettes on the mantle, and the lighter on the opposite shelf, he was forced to go stamping around the room for every new smoke. In a few days the habit was "vibrated," like the walls of Jericho, into discard.

Now that you have discovered that vibrations can tear down and that rhythms can build up, I suggest that you put all the habits that you want to cultivate, such as the habit of prayer, of sleep, of creative writing, into as regular a rhythm as possible, and any habit you wish to break try to put into a pattern of jarring vibrations as completely as you can. Just as you have regular hours each day for your meals, why not reserve a regular hour every day for your prayers?

If one can "vibrate" the walls of Jericho down, he can "rhythm" the streets of the New Jerusalem "up." I have joined friends walking around the White House and the Capitol pouring the rhythm of love and prayer out upon the occupants and I know much good can come from such efforts.

The spoken word, if spoken in anger, starts *vibrations* in the air that strike upon the tympanum of the ear of the listener where they are reconverted into sounds that strike in turn upon the heart and hurts the receiver. The loving word, on the other hand, starts rhythms in motion that carry blessings to the ears and hearts of the listeners. The telephone carries the voice much farther than the word spoken into the air alone, the radio carries it still farther, and mental telepathy carries thoughts farther and faster and in a still more mysterious way than the radio. Finally, prayer, which uses a more delicate and perfect wave length than mental telepathy or radio ever touched, carries thought and wishes farthest of all.

Elijah one day became curious to find out exactly what was the wave length of prayer that made it so much more powerful than any other form of communication. So he climbed a high mountain to discover what sort of rhythm or vibration carried prayer so far and so fast. The experiment, which ranks above Franklin's attempt to find the secret of electricity, is recorded in the 19th chapter of I Kings, the 11th and 12th verses: "And the voice said,

Go forth and stand upon the mount before the Lord. And, behold, the Lord passed by, and a great strong wind rent the mountains, and brake in pieces the rocks before the Lord; but the Lord was not in the wind: and after the wind an earthquake; but the Lord was not in the earthquake: and after the earthquake a fire; but the Lord was not in the fire: and after the fire a sound of gentle stillness." I use the alternate translation instead of "A still small voice." This experience revealed to Elijah exactly what the modern scientists have since discovered, that the shorter the wave length the farther the radio carries, likewise the softer and more still the prayer is, the more powerful are the results. All this puts a great premium upon the art of silence.

You who are reading these words please pause for a few moments at this point and listen to the sound of gentle stillness that fills the room and fills your soul. Whisper to the Lord, "Hold me in perfect alignment, oh Father, to Your heavenly will, and carry me deeply into the blessed rhythm of Your heavenly love." In answer you will hear His voice coming down the ages. "Be still and know that I am God."

CHAPTER VIII

Dynamic Symmetry in the First Five Dimensions

THE LITTLE city of Athens has astounded the world in the way its sons surpassed all mankind in philosophy (Socrates, Plato and Aristotle), in drama (Aeschylus, Sophocles and Euripides), in oratory (Demosthenes and Pericles), in architecture (the Acropolis), in military science (Miltiades), in sculpture (Phidias) and in poetry (Homer). The reason was very simple: first, they invoked divine aid before they started anything, whether it was the battle of Thermopylae, the Odyssey of Homer or Demosthenes' oration on the Crown. And second, they made rhythm the center and core of all their education. When the Greeks got these two elements perfectly blended one of the greatest discoveries of the ages burst upon them. Out of the marriage of Alignment, the masculine principle, and Rhythm, the feminine principle, was born a son known as Dynamic Symmetry.

The Egyptians whose education was also based on alignment and rhythm had made the discovery before the Greeks and upon it based their land measurements, their pyramids, their art, and finally created the greatest civilization of their day. I am not an authority on Egyptology, but I did major in Greek and can speak with special assurance when I say that as soon as the Greeks applied dynamic symmetry to their art they produced the greatest sculpture in the world. After the Greek golden age waned, the precious knowledge having been delegated to the secret masonry, the masons concealed the secret so success-fully that they lost it. Da Vinci, Dürer and the Gothic builders rediscovered it. At the end of the Renaissance it disappeared. Only a few decades ago when sculpture again came into its own it was found for the third time.

The sunflower is the most perfect example of dynamic symmetry in the plant world for it always keeps its face turned toward the sun. The seeds in this flower which thus derive their life directly from the sun, form a series of intersecting curves. Symmetry means balance and we naturally would expect these two sets of intersecting curves to contain an equal number of seeds. But nature and God do not subscribe to so mechanical a formula. The seeds on one side of the sunflower outnumber those on the other, which to all appearances is a violation of balance. Then where does the symmetry come in? Listen carefully, for here lies the Secret of the Ages:

When a sunflower is small there are 21 seeds on one side and 34 on the other. As it grows larger, there appear 34 on one side and 55 on the other; the next stage is 89 on one side and 144 on the other. In other words, the larger side regularly consists of the sum of the two sides at the former stage. The mathematical ratio of one side is always 1.618 larger than the other.

Furthermore, the distribution of leaves along the central stem also shows the same constant ratio. This orderly distribution of the leaves of plants is connected with a distinctive series of numbers 1, 2, 3, 5, 8, 13, 21, 34, 55, 89, 144, etc. known as geometric progression. One of the larger numbers in the series divided by the preceding one always equals 1.618 and this ratio explains the symmetry of the design of the plant system.

Taking their cue from nature the Greeks discovered that the square is not God's standard of beauty, but the rectangle; and the circle is not the last word in grace, but the oval. Taking the sea shell as an example of strength and beauty, note how first there is a rectangle (Figure A) where one side is 1.618 higher than it is broad. Now construct a square on the longer side keeping symmetry in the same way and you have Figure B. Then move at right angles again and you have Figure C. Give this whirling rectangle another whirl and behold how its power and

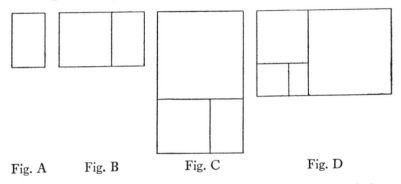

Fig. A   Fig. B   Fig. C   Fig. D

beauty grows (Figure D). Give it one more turn and then use your pen drawing curves along the diagonals of each square, starting with the first, and see what you have: the basic pattern of the chambered nautilus (Figure E). Now let God give it a whirl and the chambered nautilus itself emerges in all its perfection and beauty (See next page).

The chambered nautilus is a perfect illustration of Dynamic Symmetry. Its physical beauty is bounded by physical and mathematical law.

As this is not a book on art, I shall not try to explain the intricacies of dynamic symmetry as applied to sculpture and architecture. All I can say is that not only does the ratio of 1 to 1.618 comprise the sides and whorls of the Chambered Nautilus but likewise of the human body as expressed in the Venus di Milo and the Winged Victory of Samothrace, and rises to its greatest architectural perfection in the Greek Parthenon and some of the Gothic Cathedrals.

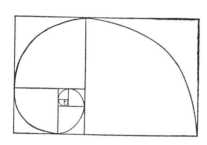

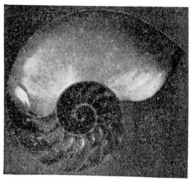

Fig. E   Chambered Nautilus

The human frame is a wonderful example of dynamic symmetry. Man, being right-handed or left-handed, one hand is 1.618 more efficient than the other. He also has two lungs, two lobes to his heart, two feet, two arms, two eyes, two nostrils, two ears. But, alas, he has only one mouth, which may account for the shallowness and worthlessness of so much of his conversation. If he looked longer at the wonders of nature and listened more to the song of the birds and talked less gossip about his neighbors he would undoubtedly be far wiser and happier.

There are two motions to one's breathing, one outward, one inward; two motions of the heart beat—and so life moves on. Athletes grow strong not through tensing the muscles alone, nor by relaxing them alone, but through a rhythmic balanced interchange between the two. Genius is developed not alone by stepping into the silence and getting still, nor by expending all one's energy from morning till night in rapturous enthusiasm, but through a balanced, rhythmic interchange between the two. And finally, the great miracles in the spiritual realm are not brought about by smug serenity in the midst of comfort and ease where disturbances never occur, but rather through the peace that passeth understanding when the turbulent waves of life are tossing the little vessel like an egg shell, and all the doors of hope seem closed.

Profound books have been inspired by the paradoxes that create dynamic symmetry in its highest form. There is such power generated in giving without being seen as the giver that a best seller was written about it, *Magnificent Obsession*. There is such power generated in being labeled as a sinner and living as a saint that a masterpiece was written about it, *Les Miserables*.

Such power is generated in being sinned against and forgiving the sinner that miracles of healing have occurred through no other act than this. Opening these doors of dynamic symmetry lets the healing power of heaven flow unobstructed into the hidden parts of the body, no matter how deep, to bring the cure. No matter how great the dream that one catches on the mountain top, it can be conveyed to those below if the dreamer can obey the laws of dynamic symmetry.

The most powerful prayer that one can pray is the one that is made up of two ingredients—one-half an ardent, sincere desire for the thing prayed for, and one-half an equally sincere relinquishing of the desire completely into the hands of the Father to grant or deny as He sees best. Abraham wished for a son but was willing to relinquish him, and as a result the son was returned to him, and through him a long line of prophets and a mighty race. Gandhi's achievements came through his practice of renunciation. He renounced leadership, and leadership beyond the dreams of men was given him; he renounced the use of physical force, and a mighty power called soul force brought most of his dreams to pass.

The secret process of how the pattern visioned on the Mount comes into manifestation on Earth, can best be clarified through the parable of the stereoscope. This instrument consists of two miniature panes of ordinary glass through which one looks—not at one picture but at two pictures of the same scene, yet pictures that are not from exactly the same point of view. One view is taken a few paces to the right of the other—we might say a modified 1 to 1.618 ratio. The pictures are similar in one respect— they are of the same scene, and dissimilar in the other respect—they are not taken from the same spot. In each case you find something negative combining with something positive, which, when your eyes get into focus (or as Jesus put it, when your eyes become single), you find yourself no longer looking at a flat picture, but through a doorway, as it were, into a new world with heights and depths and shadows. Indeed you feel tempted to step through the doorway and stroll down the country lane or city street that opens before you. In other words, a couple of two-dimensional pictures when brought into focus under the principle of dynamic symmetry opens to you a three-dimensional world.

The three greatest dramatists, Aeschylus, Sophocles and Shakespeare, were the world's most skilled users of dynamic symmetry. The Greek drama grew out of the ballad dance. In this dance, the singing and chanting chorus first moved to the right—this was called the strophe. Then they moved to the left—this was called the antistrophe. Between dances the leader of the chorus told the story. Later he became an actor and in the natural evolution of the drama the new leader of the chorus in turn also became an actor. During the height of the Greek drama there were never more than two actors on the stage at a time—always in perfect balance, usually in perfect contrast—perfect examples of dynamic symmetry.

With only two actors, and with a chorus moving rhythmically in the strophe and antistrophe, the stage was truly set for dynamic symmetry at its best. This ballad dance was not a mechanical device manufactured by the brains of men, but an organic expression springing from the deep dynamic symmetry rooted in Nature and Life.

Dr. William M. Mann, director of the National Zoological Park at Washington, D. C. and T. H. Gillespie of the Edinburgh Zoo agree that the pacings of animals back and forth in their cages are "not efforts to get out but are a form of rhythmic play or dance. A bear, for instance, will perform this dance not only when caged but will do it on a ledge of rock with nothing to confine him but his own wish to take so many steps each way. If you'll study those pacing animals, you'll see that they always take the same number of steps in each direction, make the same motion with their heads at the turn, and if they take too long a step and come out wrong, they'll mark time in order to restore the rhythm." *

Shakespeare was the most ardent and obedient disciple of dynamic symmetry of all time. The story of his development as a dramatist is fascinating. His first original play, *Love's Labor Lost,* consisted of a prince and four knights, all sworn to have nothing to do with women; and a prin-

* From: "Don't Pity the Animals in the Zoo"—Reader's Digest—March 1951.

cess and four ladies, all sworn to have nothing to do with men. The knights who had never met these women, retired for a season to the castle of the prince; the women retired to spend a period in the castle of the princess. These estates, strange to say, adjoined each other; and one by one a knight would meet, accidentally, a lady, until all had met and fallen in love. And thus the story ended and all lived happily ever after.

Shakespeare's next play was a little less "wooden" but still followed the rules of dynamic symmetry almost as faithfully as his first. In this one, *A Comedy of Errors,* a merchant of Syracuse had sons who were identical twins, and each had a servant who also were identical twins. The mother with one son and one attendant got lost on a storm-tossed sea and for years could not be found. The mixup between the two sons and the two servants, when they finally met, created the first important comedy based on mistaken identity.

In Shakespeare's *Romeo and Juliet,* the dynamic symmetry is still strongly marked but less obtrusive. Two opposing families each has one child, but one is a boy and one is a girl. When they come together Shakespeare's powers at last find their full strength; and a drama comparable to the chambered nautilus in artistic perfection is brought to birth.

Then follow the tragedies *King Lear, Hamlet* and *Macbeth,* in which the cold skeleton of dynamic symmetry is so clothed over with brilliant poetry and magnificent characterization that only an expert can detect the basic principles upon which they were built.

The moral laws of the universe are based upon dynamic symmetry. When Moses brought the Ten Commandments down from Mount Sinai they were inscribed on two tablets—not one. The first carried the five laws of man's relationship to God; the second carried the five laws of man's relationship to man. We might say that they are alike but not equal. God's laws are 1.618 greater than man's. The Two Great Commandments upon which Jesus hung all the law of the prophets are the most outstanding examples of spiritual dynamic symmetry the religious world has ever known, just as the cross furnishes its most outstanding symbol.

In my own studies in Jesus in the volume, *The Way, The Truth and The Life,* I take pains to show how beginning with the Beatitudes, the Sermon on the Mount is a perfect example of dynamic symmetry from beginning to end. Each pair of Beatitudes begets a third. The first chapter of the Sermon (Matthew V) deals entirely with man's moral responsibilities toward man, and the second chapter (Matthew VI) deals with man's moral responsibilities toward God, and the third chapter (Matthew VII) sums the first two up in such balanced symmetry as to take one's breath away.

The second third of the book I devote to Jesus' parables. And here we discover that he told *all* his parables in pairs. As Noah assembled the creatures in the ark two by two, so they could reproduce themselves, so Jesus assembled his thoughts in parables two by two in the minds and hearts of his listeners. For instance, he admonished them to count the cost of time and energy before they started the climb into the higher dimensions of the Kingdom. "This admonition," to quote from *The Way, The Truth and The Life,* (pp. 69–70) "took the form of two parables, arranged in dynamic symmetry like the stereoscopic lens, through contemplation of which one could step into a new dimension of thought and action:

"For which of you, wanting to build a tower, does not first sit down to calculate the expense, to see if he has enough money to complete it? —in case, after he has laid the foundation and then is unable to finish the building, all the spectators start to make fun of him, saying, 'This fellow started to build but he could not finish it!'"

"Or what king sets out to fight against another king without first sitting down to deliberate whether with ten thousand men he can encounter the king who is attacking him with twenty thousand? If he can not, when the other is still at a distance he will send an embassy to do homage to him."

"One can note a perfect balance and dynamic symmetry between these two parables. One parable deals with inanimate objects, the other with living men. One plans in terms of construction, the other in terms of destruction. One is concerned with projects of peace, the other with projects of war. But both represent in our day as well as in Jesus' day projects which require more careful preliminary planning than any other work we can think of. Today, before any hotel or office block is erected bids must be made and estimates considered with great care. And before an army makes an advance the preparation or logistics has to be taken care of in the most thorough of ways."

Here is another pair of parables that illustrates Jesus' use of dynamic symmetry:

"No one tears a piece from a new cloak and sews it on an old cloak; otherwise he will tear the new cloak, and the new piece will not match with the old."

"No one pours fresh wine into old wineskins; otherwise the fresh wine will burst the wineskins, the wine will be spilt and the wineskins ruined."

"Note how in the one parable there are men working at the winepress out-of-doors; and in the other there are women working on cloth indoors. One deals with wet goods, the other with dry goods; the one with something fluid to take into the body, the other with something static to *put on the outside* of the body. These parables, so completely different, focus upon one great central truth; we must not patch in a little here and patch in a little there, but we must go all the way out for God." *

Here is another pair of parables that shows God's love for men:

"Which of you with a hundred sheep, if he loses one, does not leave the ninety-nine in the open field and go after the lost one till he finds it? When he finds it, he lays it on his shoulders with joy, and when he gets home he gathers his friends and neighbors: Rejoice with me, he says to them, for I have found the sheep I lost."

"Or again, suppose a woman has ten shillings. If she loses one, does she not light a lamp and scour the house, searching carefully till she finds it? And when she finds it, she gathers her women-friends and neighbors, saying, Rejoice with me, for I have found the shilling I lost."

"Note that here is the man and woman again, one seeking an inanimate thing, one seeking a living thing, but in both cases, the little things they are seeking are perfectly helpless. The little coin cannot get up and seek its owner; neither can the baby sheep climb the mountains to find its owner. All they can do is to wait. But both are very, very precious in the sight of God. In the days of Palestine, the coins worn by a married woman were symbolical, and each one had a precious value as a part of the whole. Likewise, every good shepherd valued each sheep and he rejoiced more over the lost one that was found than over the other ninety-nine that were safe. Here we have the dynamic symmetry of the Father Love and Mother Love of God uniting to save every lost and wandering child." **

* *The Way, The Truth and The Life,* Glenn Clark. Harper's, pp. 81–82.
** *The Way, The Truth and The Life,* Glenn Clark. Harper's, pp. 85–86.

CHAPTER IX

Dynamic Symmetry in the Sixth Dimension

THE PRINCIPLE underlying all the parables of Jesus mentioned in the last chapter can be summed up in the word, polarization—the mighty, eternal, cosmic rhythm between two opposite poles, sometimes known as positive and negative, sometimes as masculine and feminine. The positive or masculine can be called the desire, the negative or feminine, the relinquishment.

The male division of the Mind is the conscious realm that conceives the idea, visions it and images it; the female division of the mind is the subconscious realm which receives ideas and believes implicitly every idea the conscious mind impresses upon it. But the subconscious mind cannot bring it into expression unless the idea is impressed upon it by the conscious mind with *feeling*. The conscious mind can think, conceive and imagine; but it cannot impress its conceptions upon the subconscious unless it *feels* them. When the conscious mind warmly *feels* these conceptions as already accomplished, not coldly *thinks* them as something merely possible of accomplishment, then the subconscious mind accepts them in their perfect completeness and gives form and expression to them.

A high type of meditation used consciously or unconsciously by the great geniuses is to move alternately from the conscious to the subconscious mind. The meditator first steps into his subconscious mind and kneels in humility and obedience to the conscious mind. Then he steps into the conscious mind and impresses affirmations and commands upon the subconscious. Then he steps back into the subconscious mind and obediently accepts these commands and affirmations in complete trust as absolute truth, and surrenders them into the hands of the Father.

The psalms sung in the orthodox churches, the affirmations of the New Thought centers, the mantrams of the eastern religions, all have the purpose of impressing, through repetition, upon the subconscious mind, the great cosmic truths of life. But if your eye is single, said Jesus, and if you really put first the Kingdom of Heaven and its righteousness, and if you accept these truths with *feeling,* loving God with all your heart and mind and soul and strength, you won't have to depend upon "many repetitions as the Gentiles do." The most effective way to reach your subconscious is not by mechanical force but through the power of faith and love, in other words through the power of sincere and exalted *feeling.*

As it is sometimes difficult to get the feeling when one is alone, Jesus offered this solution, "When two or three agree together touching anything, it will be done unto them." That explains why the most powerful of all meditations is often found where two persons of the opposite sex come together and agree; for the man to take his stand in the conscious mind with the door of love wide open into his subconscious mind; and for the woman to abide in her surrendered, obedient subconscious mind, receiving all the commands and affirmations coming from the man and surrendering them with herself into the hands of God. Instead of alternately stepping back and forth with a shifting of spiritual "gears," as is necessary when one meditates alone, there is a quiet resting, each person in the other and both in God, a constant abiding under the Shelter of the Almighty, a perfect experience of dwelling in the Secret Place of the Most High.

Parapsychology through its research in mental telepathy has proved to the world what metaphysicians have always known—that the mind of each one of us is a part of the Universal Mind. That being so, when Jesus impressed upon Mary, sitting at his feet, the great truths of the Kingdom and she was accepting them without qualification or doubt, he was, through her deep faith and love, actually reaching into the Universal Mind, and sowing seeds that would bear rich harvests in all the years that were to come. What you ask or proclaim in the secret of the inner room will be granted you openly. And thus we see the truth in Jesus' statement, "Where two agree touching anything. . . . I will be in the midst of you and all your prayers will be answered."

When a man meditates alone it is often hard to convert his cold thought into warm feeling. But when a man and woman who love each other with a high, pure love meditate together in an elevated fellowship of mutual trust, there is a heavenly interchange of strong, exalted feeling. Then all that is required is for the man to express his thoughts, his conceptions and his daydreams with perfect love and trust, and for the woman to accept them with equally perfect love and trust, and everything thus conceived and thus expressed takes permanent form and creates permanent results in the visible world. Most of the profoundest and most permanent advances in spiritual history have come to pass through such partnerships. The first perfect spiritual partnership was:

1. Jesus and Mary

The second great partnership of the Spirit was

2. Saint Francis and Saint Claire

The third was

3. Fenelon and Madame Guyon

The fourth was

4. Saint John of the Cross and Saint Teresa

The fifth was

5. Gandhi and Mira.

The service Mary rendered Jesus in accepting his visions and daydreams with the deep feeling of love and trust was infinitely more valuable in his ministry than the more obvious service rendered by Martha in serving his physical needs.

It was said that when Francis and Claire were in a room meditating and praying together, the Franciscan friars felt the power emanating from that room, and at times could almost see it as a light. But even this beautiful friendship was misunderstood at times and for that reason very rarely did they meet.

The most inspired spiritual literature of their time was produced by Fenelon and Madame Guyon. But the Bishops, not appreciating the purity of their love and fearing scandal, banished Fenelon to a little parish on the outskirts of France.

No literature since Jesus' day surpasses in Christian love the Lays and Songs of Saint John of the Cross. When he was appointed to teach the nuns in Saint Teresa's convent his power of expression flowered. The subconscious minds of Teresa and these humble nuns responded to the beautiful affirmations of his poetic mind and through their orchestration tremendous power spread through all of Spain.

What Francis and Claire did for Italy, Saint John of
the Cross and Saint Teresa did for Spain, and Fenelon
and Madame Guyon did for France.

These men, Saint Francis, Saint John and Fenelon,
were all considered saints. So were the women: Saint
Claire, Saint Teresa and Madame Guyon. In our own
day many would call Gandhi a saint. Certainly no man of
our time has accomplished such permanent results through
"soul force" and "soul force" alone as he did. One of the
keys to his tremendous powers is revealed to us in a book,
Gandhi's Letters To A Disciple, which was published
after this chapter was begun.

As we do not have the detailed story of the other partnerships let us accept this as typical of them all. In his
introduction to the book John Haynes Holmes writes:

"The Gandhi-Mira episode is one of the great idyllic
stories of human life. It has always suggested to me the
story which must have attached to Jesus' relations with
the high-minded and heroic women who clustered about
Him in His ancient ministry in Palestine. In the final
crisis of His career, when the Nazarene was arrested,
tried and crucified, these women remained faithful to
Him even when all His disciples excepting only John had
fled away. This utter loyalty in death must have been the
reflection of the similar loyalty of these women in life.
They followed Jesus and served Him because they saw in
Him the Master. So it was with Mira, who saw in Gandhi
the Mahatma.

"In her Preface to this volume Mira tells the dramatic
tale of her discovery of Gandhi and its cataclysmic influence upon her life. She was an English girl, Madeleine
Slade, daughter of a distinguished British admiral, a pop-

ular social figure, highly educated, tall, beautiful, proud of bearing, with glowing eyes and liquid voice. Early enraptured by music, she was drawn to Romain Rolland by his writings on Beethoven, 'and through Romain Rolland to Bapu,' whose biography the great Frenchman had written. Mira read this book and said, 'From that moment I knew that my life was dedicated to Bapu.'

"Mira herself speaks of her experience as 'a power' that was 'impelling' her before she knew either Rolland or Gandhi; in the former case it gave her 'an extraordinary sense of mellow happiness,' and in the latter case, burst forth into a light which, like the dawn, 'glowed brighter and brighter in my heart,' and at last became as 'the Sun of Truth pouring his rays into my soul.'

"The most remarkable part of her experience is what she did with it. Had it been mere emotionalism of a romantic type, Mira would have rushed to Gandhi, if only to indulge her sentimental intoxication. But she did nothing of the sort. She did not even go to India, to meet him and sit adoringly at his feet. She did not even write him, or communicate with him in any way. With amazing sanity and self-control she set herself to the business of preparation, both physical and spiritual, for her task of dedication to the great Indian leader. This involved training in as apparently trivial an exercise as sitting cross-legged on the floor, and in as definitely important a one as diet and knowledge of Hindu literature. Only when she had completed almost a year of intense concentration and hard labor, did she feel herself fit to come into Gandhi's presence and offer him the service of her life. Deeply touching is the scene of her meeting with the Mahatma. 'I could see and feel nothing but a heavenly light,' she writes. 'He lifted me up and taking me in his arms said, "You shall be my daughter." And so has it been from that day.'

"There can be no doubt as to the nature of this episode. It is the religious ecstasy of the highest and purest character. It is the soul obedient to God, and to His servant. It is the making of oneself a servant of truth and light. There have been many other instances of this spiritual surrender to so exalted a saint as Gandhi.

"Mira was changed in an instant—not by any sentiment of passion, but by a capture of her whole life by the subduing power of the spirit. God spoke in the sudden disclosure of Gandhi to his disciple, and Mira had the courage, and the supreme intelligence, to answer. Her life therewith became exalted, and to the end as beautiful as a gift laid upon an altar."

Then follow the letters, 220 pages of them—and all by Gandhi. "These letters," writes Mira, "are a selection of 351 out of 650 which I collected and treasured year by year. In the days of arrests and imprisonments, with their accompanying searches and destruction of papers, my only anxiety was for Bapu's letters. Whenever I saw the likelihood of arrest approaching, I would leave them with some 'unsuspected' friend, or in some institute where no searches would be likely to be made. Then, for the last three years, I have kept them with me in a little tin trunk. Mercifully they have survived all vicissitudes, and now, when they are at last published, I shall feel an immense sense of relief. The treasure of spiritual thought and guidance which they contain, though addressed only to one, must be available to all."

As one reads these letters he can imagine he is also reading the letters of Saint Francis to Saint Claire, of

Saint John to Teresa, and of Fenelon to Madame Guyon. Tremendous dynamic symmetry of the upper dimensions was released through the lives of these men through the pure adoration and loving service of these women. Mira closes the book as follows:

"On January 30, at about 7:30 P.M. the news of the assassination was brought to me in Pashulok. I had come out on the verandah. As I heard the words, I became motionless and gazing up into the sky saw the stars glittering above the forest trees. The only words which spoke in my heart were: 'Bapu, Bapu, so it has come!' And with that there came a sense of peace which surmounted even the blinding shock.

"For me there were only two, God and Bapu. And now they have become one!

"When I heard the news something deep, deep down within me opened—the door to the imprisoned soul—and Bapu's spirit entered there. From that moment a new sense of the eternal abides with me.

"Though Bapu's beloved physical presence is no longer with us, yet his sacred spirit is even nearer. Sometimes Bapu had said to me, 'When my body is no more there will not be separation, but I shall be nearer to you. The body is a hindrance.' I listened in faith. Now I know, through experience, the divine truth of these words."

And so Mira stepped into the glorious dynamic symmetry of the seventh dimension in this realm of time as Gandhi stepped into it over there in the realm of Eternity.

Again we see, in inspired literature, the work of the conscious and subconscious mind working together through men and women. The friendship of Dante and Beatrice was so platonic and spiritual that it never attracted criticism although some undiscerning readers may misunderstand it. But it did lead to the writing of one of the greatest masterpieces of literature of all time—the allegory of the human soul in its journey from hell to heaven.

The love of Robert Browning and Elizabeth Barrett became a living prayer partnership that led to the finest poetry of their day. This was the most perfect married partnership among all the literary folk that ever lived.

It has been rare that such ideal marriages occurred among spiritual leaders. Socrates had his Xantippe and John Wesley and scores of others had wives who could not orchestrate with them in spiritual meditation. The one outstanding exception is Jonathan Edwards whose wife was in utter accord with his spiritual vision. The result was something permanent in two fields: first, a family of children whose descendants have been prominent in moulding the destiny of America; and second, a philosophy on the place of freedom of the will that stands as the masterpiece of his age.

Unfortunately, all through time men have failed to understand this need and its fulfillment. It was not something that required marriage; there was Dante and Beatrice. And, of course, misused, there was danger of sorrow and tragedy, as in the partnerships of Shelley and Mary Godwin. Even when high and perfect it was often misunderstood. But out of all this evidence of the past the truth remains that the most creative meditation is where two come together and agree in the spirit of love and trust, which constitutes "praying in Jesus' name," one a man who images his dreams and one a woman who receives them in complete trust and passes them on to the Lord. Out of this perfect orchestration of thinking and feeling and sharing with God, wonderful things have been born on this planet. An outstanding student of spiritual biographies has reported that every spiritual leader who has left permanent results had a wife who trusted and loved completely as Jonathan Edwards and Browning had, or a Beatrice or Mira who gave spiritual feeling as she received his visions with perfect love and perfect trust.

Thus we see what a significant place *feeling* has when expressed in the form of dynamic symmetry in the lives of men and women. One of the essential elements is contrast, which is the very core of dynamic symmetry, and dynamic symmetry is not limited to sex. Some of the most powerful spiritual partnerships have been between men of opposite types such as Goethe and Schiller, and Carlyle and Emerson. When I, a teacher of literature in a northern college and a member of the white race, made a pilgrimage to meet Dr. George Washington Carver, a teacher of science in the deep south, a member of the black race, a spiritual partnership was established between us which both of us agreed doubled our creative output for the next ten years. Now that he and God have become one, I sometimes feel the partnership more vitally than ever.

Dynamic symmetry of the sixth dimensional type is found in powerful expression in poetry 'drawn out' of the writer by the ones he wrote it for, as Julia Ward Howe's "Battle Hymn of the Republic"; and in orators inspired by the audiences that welcome them. Indeed, nowhere is dynamic symmetry more potently operative than in the field of oratory. Someone has said that no great orator was ever created without a great audience. A hostile or luke-warm congregation will "kill" an oration almost as surely as frost will kill an opening blossom. Jesus experienced this when he could do no mighty works in his

home town because of their unbelief. He was referring to
this when he told his apostles in his final instructions
before sending them forth to address many cities:

"If they receive you as a righteous man (one who can
give them a commonplace sermon on how to be good)
they will receive a righteous man's reward; but if they
receive you as a prophet (one through whom God speaks
a message) they will receive a prophet's reward." In other
words the attitude of the audience will modify the quality
of eloquence or lack of eloquence of the speaker. If they
come in coldness they will receive information; if they
come with warmth they will receive inspiration, and, if
the speaker is a clear enough channel, actual revelation.

There was one dramatic moment in spiritual history
when a group larger than two or three stepped into that
complete, perfect orchestration of souls, all of one mind,
gathered in one place, and that was called Pentecost, the
place where the sixth and seventh dimensions became one.

CHAPTER X

Dynamic Symmetry in the Seventh Dimension

AND NOW we stand in the midst of the seventh dimension. Let us pause for a moment and listen to the voice of Jesus describing it: Lay not up for yourselves treasures in the third dimension of the earth, but lay up for yourselves treasures in the seventh dimension of heaven. If you once reach this seventh dimensional area, he concluded in effect, "all these things shall be added unto you." And the Psalmist completes the picture: "Because thou hast made the Lord even the Most High thy habitation there shall no evil befall thee, neither shall any plague come nigh thy dwelling."

If we can find the right dynamic symmetry of the seventh dimension all things shall be added unto us as is verified by these seven major promises of Jesus:

1. And whatsoever ye shall ask in my name, that will I do. (John 14:13)
2. If two of you shall agree on earth as touching anything that they shall ask it shall be done for them of my Father which is in heaven. (Matthew 18:19)
3. If you have faith as a grain of mustard seed ye shall say to this mountain, "Remove hence to yonder place" and it shall remove, and nothing shall be impossible to you. (Matthew 17:20)
4. If you abide in me and my words abide in you, ye may ask whatsoever ye will and it will be given unto you. (John 15:7)

5. Everyone that asketh receiveth; and he that seeketh findeth; and to him that knocketh it shall be opened. (Matthew 7:8)

6. When thou has shut thy door, pray to thy Father which is in secret; and thy Father which seeth in secret shall reward thee openly. (Matthew 6:6)

7. He that believeth on me the works that I do shall he do also, and greater works than these shall he do, because I go unto my Father. (John 14:12)

These promises *seem* impossible. But all impossible things are possible if one can find the Key. And the Key to these seven *promises* lies hidden in these seven *paradoxes:*

1. The last shall be first. (Matthew 19:30)

2. Whosoever shall smite thee on thy right cheek, turn to him the other also. (Matthew 5:39)

3. Do good to them that hate you, and pray for them which despitefully use you. (Matthew 5:44)

4. Blessed are the meek for they shall inherit the earth. (Matthew 5:5)

5. Blessed are the poor in spirit for theirs is the Kingdom of Heaven. (Matthew 5:3)

6. Whosoever wants to be great among you must be your servant, and whoever wants to hold the first place among you must be your slave. (Matthew 20:27–28)

7. He that findeth his life shall lose it, and he that loseth his life for my sake shall find it. (Matthew 10:39)

"A paradox" said Frank Olmstead, "is a phenomenon on the boundary of a new dimension." And the boundary where all of Jesus' paradoxes lead us is straight into the seventh dimension—in other words, into the Kingdom of Heaven itself.

Therefore, all of the promises listed on the preceding page, extravagant as they may seem, become possible whenever one learns how to practice the paradoxes given above. But before we can practice them we must understand them.

Remember how the foundation of all dynamic symmetry rests on the one hand upon the Law of Alignment, and, on the other hand, upon the Law of Rhythm? The last of the paradoxes listed contains the last word in the Law of Rhythm, and the next to the last contains the last word in the Law of Alignment.

Let us consider first of all the Law of Rhythm. Where all vibrations are resolved into rhythms and all rhythms into stillness, "the sound of gentle stillness" or "the still small voice," there we experience rhythm at its finest and highest. When any one on this earth becomes so still, so at peace, so completely liberated from all thoughts of self, so completely immersed in God that he experiences the peace that passeth understanding, then the Rhythm from above becomes so irresistible that no evil powers on this earth can stand before it. Saint Paul who almost single-handed planted the roots of the Christian Church so deeply that they will never die, gave the finest expression of this stillness in the classic words, "I am crucified in Christ. I live and yet not I but Christ in me." The dynamic power in Saint Paul's life came from his discovery that there is no stillness like the stillness that is created by the dying to self.

So powerful is this paradox, "he that loseth his life . . . shall find it," that some branches of the Christian Church have adopted a sacrament to symbolize it in the form of complete immersion at the time of baptism. In this sacrament the initiate is bodily "drowned" for a moment. The place where he was visible a moment before suddenly becomes vacant. Only after that complete erasure of the physical form is he "resurrected"—a supposedly new creature reborn in Christ Jesus. Thus we see that the secret door to the most powerful Rhythm man can ever hope to attain is concealed in the greatest paradox Jesus ever uttered, "He that would save his life shall lose it and he who would lose his life shall save it." In other words, when one takes his own little rhythm out of the way, the mighty Rhythm of Christ comes in. Whether one describes it as "the sound of gentle stillness" or "the peace that passeth understanding," it matters not; the Power is there!

When we turn from the Law of Rhythm to the Law of Alignment we encounter another paradox of Jesus, "Whosoever wants to be great among you must be your servant, and whosoever wants to hold first place among you must be your slave."

Alignment as we have already learned consists of putting first things first, the lower always subordinate to the higher. All cannot take the front seats, some must take the back seats or confusion will reign. As too many cooks spoil the broth, it is equally true that too many leaders will bring any movement or any institution into chaos. If all tried to lead an army, bedlam would be the result. Let the natural leaders lead, implied Jesus. Take the back seats, be willing to accept the leadership of any who are better equipped to lead than you are, and, just as water flows into the lowliest valleys, you may find the leadership "gravitating" to you. For the truest paradox ever uttered was, "The meek shall inherit the earth."

When a guide escorts you through an art gallery, you let him direct you, you don't try to direct him. Every man you meet is superior to you in at least one respect, and those willing to bow down in affairs where they are not supposed to lead are the ones who will be chosen to lead where God wants them to lead. Thus we find that as the quintessence of Rhythm is death, the quintessence of

Alignment is slavery. Strange, isn't it, that the two words mankind abhors the most are presented by Jesus as the most powerful doorways to spiritual power open to man!

But while the paradox of dying has been given expression in the church in the sacrament of baptism by immersion, there has been no sacrament as yet adequate to give full expression to the paradox of slavery. It is true that some of the smaller denominations, as well as the Catholics, undertake to meet this lack in such rituals as the sacrament of washing the feet. But would it not be possible to adopt a sacrament in our churches that would go still farther than that—a sacrament which, if entered into sincerely and humbly, might release power second only to the sacrament of the Lord's Supper? Let us imagine an entire congregation coming to kneel at the altar rail as is the custom of most denominations in the administration of the Holy Communion, and each one extending his hands while the pastor or priest moves from one to the other, carrying, instead of the wafers and the cup, a ribbon of pure white with which he momentarily binds each pair of wrists as he pronounces the words, "He that would be first shall be as a servant, and he that would be greatest of all shall be as a slave." As he passes rapidly from one to another, each one emptying himself as a vacant vessel before the Lord, such a current of power from on high would sweep through the kneeling congregation that the whole community would be transformed by its power. Because pride, vanity and ego are the greatest blocks to the spiritual life today, I know of no ritual that would release greater spiritual power than one such as this.

Having learned that one cannot enter into the Kingdom of Heaven of the seventh dimension by thought only but by Grace; and that the Grace of God is most ready to act through the doorways of Death or Slavery, a group of very devout and surrendered souls experimented with the sacrament described above and the results were tremendous. Five of them, for instance, after sharing in the ritual of becoming slaves of Christ, broadcast a prayer for Hitler that actually stopped him in his tracks before World War II began. I describe this incident in *A Man's Reach*. So profoundly do I believe Jesus' promise that "the meek shall inherit the earth" that I actually believe (yes, *know*) that if some way could be arranged whereby three million so-called Christians could actually become aware of the reality and the joy of being slaves to Christ, we could see Christ positively inheriting the earth. Yes, I don't just believe, I *know* that under such conditions "His Kingdom would come and His will would be done on earth as it is in Heaven." This could easily be accomplished when the dynamic symmetry of Heaven, experienced through Alignment and Rhythm lifted to their highest power in the form of Death to the ego and Slavery of the outer self to the inner Christ, took control of sufficient numbers of the children of men.

I know that it was not until I had completely erased my own little self through the door of alignment into utter surrender and through the door of rhythm into complete erasure of self, that I was able to rise into the glory and bliss and marvelous power of the fifth, sixth and seventh dimensions. It was then that I experienced the ecstasy of stepping into oneness with God, my fellow men, and my Divine Plan. Since then I have knelt in spirit before every audience I speak to, and before every reader who opens my books. And I have lost all fear of death since I learned that no evil has any power in the face of one who willingly permits the little self-centered self to die, to be erased, to vanish into its native nothingness. For I learned that the redeemed Self, hidden with Christ in God, always rises from the ashes of that lesser self when it has died.

And so we find Schweitzer, dying to his great leadership in philosophy, religion and music in Europe, and humbling himself as a slave and servant to the needs of the least of those in darkest Africa, lighting a torch that will never go out! And we see Mira, dying to the great wealthy, prominent girl known as Madeleine Slade and becoming a slave to the Father of Lights shining through the Bapu in a secluded village of India, helping furnish the wave-length for the power of heaven itself to flow through and set India free.

When one is so utterly aligned with the Most High that he becomes a slave of Christ, and has put himself in such perfect rhythm with the Holy Spirit that his little self dies before the Greater Self, then there stands revealed the most powerful dynamic symmetry in all the universe. One who has passed through this process rises from death to eternal life, and from slavery to becoming a Son of God.

The opposite poles in this celestial new dynamic symmetry consist of God reaching down to man on the one hand, and man reaching up to God on the other. This is the perfect union described by Luther. "We are united as a bride is united with a husband." This union is elaborated by Rufus Moseley in his book, "Perfect Everything" where he writes, "We become flesh of His flesh, blood of His blood, soul of His soul, spirit of His spirit, life of His life." This "union of interchange" as Rufus Moseley calls it, brings into manifestation the highest form of dynamic symmetry available to man—the paradox that sums up all the lesser paradoxes. In this divine Rhythm of the seventh dimension the Lord permits us to exchange our sins for His forgiveness, our weakness for His strength, our humility for His glory, our fear for His courage, our despair for His peace, our sorrow for His joy, our infirmities for His wholeness, our impurity for His purity, our poverty for His riches, our discord for His harmony, our ignorance for His wisdom, our sordidness for His saintliness, our humanity for His divinity, our mortality for His immortality.

But alas, it is easier for a camel to go through the eye of a needle than for most people to understand the deep paradoxes: that slavery leads to dominion, captivity to freedom, and death to eternal life here and now!

It requires a seer to vision these paradoxes, a sage to understand them, and a saint to practice them. If you would add the prophet to this list his job would be to promulgate them. Verily, if enough of us saw them, understood them, practiced them, as well as preached them, the Kingdom of Heaven would be brought from invisibility into visibility upon this earth.

CHAPTER XI

Dynamic Symmetry in the Bible

ABRAHAM is the first man in the Bible who did everything the Lord commanded him to do. He lived so
completely in alignment with God in the seventh dimension that when told to leave the greatest civilization of
his day, the Sumerian in the land of Ur, and go into a
land he knew not of, he proceeded to go with perfect
trust; and when his longed-for son finally came, he was
willing at the Lord's command to prepare to sacrifice him
upon the altar.

As reward for this perfect obedience in leaving the
land of Ur he was given a better land. "I will give you
and your descendants after you the land where you are
residing, the whole of the land of Canaan, as a possession
for all time." And his complete relinquishing of Isaac led
to the return of Isaac and through him a mighty race:
"Look up to the sky and number the stars if you can. Such
shall be the number of your descendants. I have appointed
you to be father of many a nation."

Abraham also lived so completely in rhythm with his
fellowmen in the sixth dimension that every act he did
squared with the Golden Rule, "Do unto others as you
would have them do unto you." When, for instance, the
land was not equal to pasture both his and Lot's herds, he

let Lot take the rich Jordan valley land and he went to the land of the Canaanites; and when Sodom was doomed to destruction he pled with the angels to save it even if only ten good men could be found in it.

Abraham had a unique experience in the fifth dimension also, when, following an intense appeal for the Lord to send him a son, he fell into a trance, and the Lord foretold the enslavement of his descendants by the Egyptians long centuries ahead. The most comforting prophecies that sprang from the patterns of the fifth dimension were that his descendants would be in number like the stars and that the land of Canaan would be theirs.

The special trusted servant that Abraham sent back to his own people to find a wife for his son, Isaac, had evidently caught the contagion of his master's faith. He stepped into the fifth dimension and asked the Lord to give him definite guidance as to which girl drawing water from the well would be the right one. "Here I stand beside the fountain! The daughters of the citizens are coming out to draw water. Now may the maiden to whom I say, 'Pray lower your pitcher, that I may drink,' the maiden who answers, 'Drink, and let me give a drink to your camels also'—may she be the maiden thou hast allotted to thy servant Isaac! So shall I know that thou hast been kind to my master." Rebecca arrived and stepped into the pattern so completely that that marriage was arranged in heaven—the most idyllic, though brief, courtship in the Old Testament.

Esau, the eldest son of Isaac, lived in the purely material level of the third dimension, descending in times of weakness even to the jungle appetite of the second dimension. His twin brother, Jacob, on the other hand, put himself in absolute alignment with the higher unseen things, preferring such intangibles as "birthrights" and "bless-ings" over things of the flesh.

Where Jacob fell short of attaining complete dynamic symmetry was his failure to keep in rhythm in as honest a way with his fellowmen as he kept in alignment in a worshipful way with God. While he achieved real *align-ment* to the *right ends,* he failed to keep in *rhythm* with the *right means.* While he achieved the birthright and the blessing, he obtained each through craft, and for this he had to pay with interest when his Uncle Laban applied a similar trick on him in working him fourteen years in-stead of seven to get Rachel.

It was not until Jacob reached his dark hour when news that his avenging brother with armed horsemen was com-ing rapidly toward him that he stepped into such align-ment with God and such rhythm with his brother and all mankind that the resultant dynamic symmetry brought to an end the life-time feud between the two brothers, and a crowning success to his life. A night of wrestling with the Lord brought him into such heavenly alignment that he received God's blessing; and by sending loving gifts to his brother he created such heavenly rhythm that between the two all hate and resentment was swept away. To make atonement for his early failure to walk in honest rhythm with his brother, however, he was doomed to walk the rest of his life with an unrhythmic limp.

Joseph is the perfect example of how irresistible a man of destiny can become who lives, moves and has his being in the fifth dimension. Through dreams and the capacity to interpret dreams, he was able to rise continually above the vicissitudes of the second and third dimension where his associates lived, and sculpture his destiny according to the perfect pattern, eternal, infinite and unchangeable, carved for him "on the mount." Just as Moses received the *laws* of God in sets of pairs (five commandments on our duty to God and five on our duty to men) ; and just as Jesus presented the *Grace* of God in the form of parables in sets of pairs, so all of Joseph's dreams came in pairs. Through the stereoscopic lens of these pairs of dreams the perfect picture of Joseph's perfect destiny unfolded:

The first set got him into trouble:

"Joseph said to his brothers, 'Do listen to this dream I have had. Me thought, as we were binding sheaves in the field, my sheaf stood up, while your sheaves all around did homage to it!' His brothers answered, 'And are you to be king over us? You to lord it over us!' They hated him worse than ever, for what he dreamed and what he said."

"He had another dream which he told his brothers. 'Listen,' he said, 'I have had another dream! The sun, the moon and the eleven stars were doing homage to me!' When he told this to his father and his brothers, his father reproved him saying, 'What is this dream of yours? Am I and your mother and your brothers actually to bow before you to the earth?' "

The jealousy these dreams stirred in the brothers led to their selling him into slavery. Later on when he was cast into another form of bondage another pair of dreams brought him liberation, recorded as follows:

Joseph asked two fellow-prisoners, the cup-bearer and the baker of the king, "Why are you looking so downcast today?" "We have had a dream," they said, "and there is no one to interpret it." Joseph answered, "Do not interpretations belong to God? But pray tell me the dream."

"So the chief cup-bearer told Joseph his dream. 'In my dream,' he said, 'there was a vine in front of me and on the vine there were three branches. It seemed to bud, its blossoms opened, and the clusters produced ripe grapes. As the Pharaoh's cup was in my hand, I plucked the grapes, squeezed them into the Paraoh's cup, and handed the cup to the Pharaoh.' 'Here is the interpretation,' said Joseph, 'the three branches are three days. Within three days the Pharaoh will release you and restore you to your post; and you will hand the Pharaoh his cup as you used to do when you were his cup-bearer. But remember me when all goes well with you; do me the kindness of mentioning my name to the Pharaoh and get me out of here. For I was really kidnapped from the land of the Hebrews and I have done nothing in this country for which I should be put in the dungeon.' "

"When the head baker saw that the interpretation was favourable, he said to Joseph, 'In my dream I too saw something; three baskets of white bread were on my head; in the top basket there were all sorts of pastry for the Pharaoh, but the birds kept eating them out of the basket on my head.' 'Here is the interpretation,' said Joseph, 'the three baskets are three days. Within three days the Pharaoh will release you, and hang you on a tree, till the birds eat the flesh of you.' "

On the third day, which was the Pharaoh's birthday, he held a banquet for all his courtiers, and he did release the chief cup-bearer and the head baker. The chief cup-bearer he restored to his post, where he handed the cup to the Pharaoh; but the head baker he hanged. It was as Joseph had interpreted to them.

Two years later Pharaoh had two dreams. Not a one of the magicians and sages of Egypt could interpret them. Then the cup-bearer remembered the Hebrew youth and Joseph was summoned: "I have had a dream," said the Pharaoh to Joseph, "and there is no one to interpret it; but I have heard about you, that you can interpret a dream whenever you hear it." "Not I!" said Joseph to the Pharaoh; "it is God's answer that will answer the Pharaoh."

"Then the Pharaoh said to Joseph, 'In my dream I was standing on the bank of the Nile; up came seven cows from the Nile, plump and sleek, and they grazed in the

reed-grass. After them seven other cows came up, starved and very ugly and lean,—I never saw such poor cows in all the land of Egypt. The lean and ugly cows ate up the first seven plump cows, and even after they had eaten them—they were still ugly as before. Then I woke up.' "

" 'I also saw in a dream seven full ripe ears sprouting on a single stalk. Seven ears sprang up after them, withered, thin, and the thin ears swallowed up the seven ripe ears! I told all this to the magicians but not one of them could tell me the meaning.' "

Joseph said to the Pharaoh, "The Pharaoh's dreams mean one thing. God has been showing the Pharaoh what He is about to do; the seven good cows are seven years, and the seven good ears are seven years . . . it is one and the same dream. The seven lean and ugly cows that came up afterwards are also seven years, and so are the seven empty ears blasted by the east wind; there are to be seven years of famine. *The dream was doubled* for the Pharaoh because *this is fixed by God,* and ere long God will bring it about."

In Chapter 8 I said that dynamic symmetry was first discovered in Egypt. When Joseph said, "The dream was doubled . . . because this was fixed by God" he revealed that he understood this law perfectly. Through the double lens of the stereoscope of dynamic symmetry he was able to foresee not only the peril that "was fixed by God" awaiting Egypt in the future but the exact way to meet and overcome the peril. Without hesitation he gave the Pharaoh a complete blueprint of everything he should do. "Put a shrewd, intelligent man in control of all of Egypt with food-controllers throughout the country to gather and store sufficient grain of good years to carry the nation safely through the poor years."

The Pharaoh at once decided that this "shrewd, intelligent" young man who functioned in higher dimensions was exactly the one to put in charge of the nation. The Scriptures tell how he did so and how the nation was saved. Is that a suggestion our government might heed in our hours of crisis today?

Great as Joseph proved as an administrator, Moses was still greater. Moses was the most perfect 'law-giver the world has ever known, and that was because he put himself in perfect alignment with God, and moved in perfect rhythm with men. His career carried him through all the dimensions from the lowest to the highest. As a babe in the bulrushes his survival came through his one-dimensional, single-minded seeking of nourishment at his mother's breast (she masquerading as his nurse). In the two-dimensional level he killed an Egyptian in a fit of anger, and in a fit of fear fled the country. On the third-dimensional level he had access to the ancient wisdom of Egypt which was not limited to the third dimension, but went soaring up into the fourth and fifth. The forty years of sojourn in the wilderness as a shepherd gave him quiet spaces to rise up into the fourth, fifth, sixth and especially the seventh dimension, where he found union with God at the historic episode of the burning bush. As the bush was filled with fire without being consumed, Moses was "incandescent" enough to sustain the presence of God without being destroyed. The modern counterpart of the burning bush is the incandescent light bulb, so empty of air of this world that it can hold the mighty voltage of light created in the high hills.

The power in Moses was the same as that in Paul, "My strength is made perfect in (your) weakness." Moses was a poor orator; Aaron had to do the speaking for him. He had no talents with the exception of his immense capacity for selflessness. "As meek as Moses" became a by-word in the land. He alone became incandescent enough to hold the light of God.

When he returned to the court of Pharaoh facing the same task which Gandhi faced five thousand years later —to set his people free—he carried with him the power of the seventh dimension. He had risen so high that he was able to "come up over" every situation so completely that he could flow down over his foes and "overcome" them. But as Pharaoh, with the support of his magicians and sages, was ready to do battle with him on the level of the fourth dimension—the psychic level of hypnotism and magic—he boldly descended to that level and beat them at their own game. When his wand turned into a snake and swallowed all the magicians' wands, which had also turned into snakes, and when the floods of frogs and gnats and hail began to come, Moses was surpassing the power of the Hopi Indians whose invocations bring down rain, and the Hawaiian Kahunas whose invocations enable them to walk unharmed on heated stones.

The Ark of the Covenant, constructed on the lines of dynamic symmetry, was the ordained vessel for the safe-keeping of the Ten Commandments. Whenever the Israelites made camp in their marching through the wilderness they placed the Levite tribe in the center and in their midst raised the tabernacle, and in the Holy of Holies within the Tabernacle placed this sacred symbol of the soul of Israel—the Ark of the Covenant. As long as this rested at the heart and center of the nation all went well. Any nation that stole it found the curse of God was upon them, just as it falls on anyone who would appropriate another man's divine plan for himself. The Ark of the Covenant thus became the sacred symbol of the Old Testament as the Cross has become the sacred symbol of the New Testament. These two symbols create the greatest dynamic symmetry in religious history. They were alike in one respect, they represented the most sacred value respectively of Judaism and of Christianity, and that value summed up in one phrase was *alignment or union with God and rhythm of love and justice toward men.* But they were exactly opposite or at right angles to each other in another respect—the Ark (as its prototype, Noah's Ark) was built to protect and conserve that sacred value through Law; the Cross was built to sacrifice and expend that sacred value through Love. The emphasis of one was to keep, the other was to give. "He who would save his life," rings the paradox of Jesus, "shall lose it."

After the dark centuries when the Israelites had no leader save when an occasional Jeptha, Gideon or Samson would arise to rescue them, Samuel, the prophet, finally arose to power. From the moment of his pre-natal ordination by Hannah and its confirmation by the Voice calling him as a child, Samuel was open to the seventh dimension. But as his leadership became more and more a political one, he spent more and more of his time in the third dimension of practical politics, rising only rarely to the level of the fourth dimension—at which times he revealed his remarkable gift of telepathy. "Your asses have been found," he said to Saul. He also had gifts of clairvoyance in the fifth dimension when he foretold the doom, first of Eli and his sons, and later of Saul and his sons.

Next we come to Elijah and Elisha, with names so much alike and yet different, with twin miracles of bringing boys back to life and multiplying housewives' supplies of oil, thus making a perfect "dynamic symmetry team" in themselves. In Elisha, especially (particularly in I Kings, chapters 4, 5, and 6) we run the entire gamut of the seven dimensions. In the fourth dimension Elisha was one of the greatest mind-readers of all time. He read the mind

of his servant like a book when Gehazi intrigued from
Naaman the reward that he, himself, had declined, and
he read the minds of the Syrian generals, hundreds of
miles away, when they plotted ambushes for the Israelites.
He stepped into the fifth dimension when he pointed out
to his servant the horses and chariots of the Lord descending the mountain—the divine pattern of protection God
had prepared for them in the mount. He stepped into the
seventh dimension when he prayed to the Lord to save the
city through temporarily blinding the enemy. Following
this he stepped down into the third dimension and revealed his clever mind when with debonair audacity he
outfoxed the blinded leaders. "This is not the way over
the city. Follow me and I will bring you to the man whom
you seek." He led them into Samaria where the king of
Israel's army was ready to surround them. Thereupon the
king said, "My father, shall I slay them, shall I slay
them?" In response Elisha stepped into the sixth and
seventh dimensions of forgiveness and love for his enemies
and said, "Set bread and water before them that they may
eat and drink and go to their master." "So he prepared for
them a great feast," "and the marauding Aramean bands
came no more into the land of Israel."

If Jacob and Elisha, before the days of Jesus, found the
seventh dimension the only way of permanently ending
feuds and war, why can't we, as a Christian nation, at
least *try* the way that Jesus commanded us to follow?

The major and the minor prophets that came after this
Elijah-Elisha team functioned in the fifth dimension
when they were able to read the handwriting on the wall
as Daniel did, or foresee the coming calamity as Jeremiah
did, or prophesy the coming of the Messiah as Isaiah did.
They functioned in the sixth dimension when they ap-

pealed for justice to the poor and oppressed in the voice of Amos, and for mercy in the voice of Hosea, and for social reform in the voice of Isaiah and Jeremiah. Finally, they lived, moved and had their being in the seventh dimension when they put themselves in such complete alignment with God that they could thunder with authority time after time, *"Thus saith the Lord!"*

Jesus lived, moved and had his being so completely in the seventh dimension, in his unlimited, all-out, complete love for God and oneness with him; and in the sixth dimension, in his love for men and his unlimited compassion for them, that his excursions into the lower dimensions were mere passing incidents in his life. At the beginning of his ministry, for instance, he made the casual remark to Philip that Nathaniel was an Israelite in whom there was no guile. When asked how he knew the nature of one he had never seen before he replied, "While you were still under that fig tree, before Philip called you, I saw you." Nathaniel answered him, "Rabbi, you are the son of God! You are the king of Israel!" Jesus answered him, "Because I said to you, I saw you under the fig tree, do you believe me? You shall see greater things than these." And he said to him, "Truly, truly, I say to you you will see heaven opened and the angels of God ascending and descending upon the son of man."

In other words, reading the mind of another in the fourth dimension is nothing compared to receiving the inspired revelations of God in the seventh dimension. There are only a few instances where Jesus seemed to step for a moment into the third dimension where all of us humans spend most of our time: when he exclaimed in disgust over his disciples' failure to heal the epileptic, "How long must I bear with you?", when he wept over the death of Lazarus, when he agonized in the garden of Gethsemane.

But far above the few moments of this minor key we hear the great organ notes—"Peace be still." "Take no anxious thought for the morrow." "Let not your heart be troubled. Ye believe in the Father, believe also in me." "In the world ye have trouble, but take courage, I have overcome the world."

FOREWORD TO PART III

Having discovered in Part I and II the beautiful patterns of goodness, truth and beauty awaiting us in the fifth dimension; and having caught a glimpse of the ecstatic orchestration of love and harmony awaiting us in the sixth dimension; and having taken steps toward the blissful union with the Father awaiting us in the seventh dimension, the Big question that faces us now is how can we bring all these priceless treasures into practical manifestation down where we live today, in ways that will make our lives and the lives of our friends richer and finer.

When Peter reached his highest level at the Mount of Transfiguration he didn't want to come down again. "Let the world go hang" was his sentiment; "let us build three tabernacles and stay here." I have been told that the Hindu masters, when they succeed in attaining union with the Absolute, withdraw as hermits and let the world drown in its own tears. They would transcend but not transform this mortal world.

That is not the purpose of this book. Its first purpose is to show how we can *transcend* the limitations of this world; but its final purpose is to show how we can *transform* the limitations of this world.

When Jesus commissioned his disciples to go forth and "preach the gospel, heal the sick, and cast out demons,"

he meant what he said. He didn't mean for his ministers
to preach the gospel and stop there. Over and over again
he reiterated "Blessed are those who hear these words of
mine and *do* them . . . by their fruits ye shall know
them." Jesus never meant for our application of his teachings to end with the Sabbath Day. Jesus' religion was for
every day—something we should carry into our business
office, our kitchen and our athletic field. His promise,
"Whatsoever ye ask in my name" is just as applicable to
the problems of healing and guidance and friendship and
finance as it is to the problems of the church. To him, they
were one and the same.

One thing that has deterred religious leaders of the
Evangelical churches from following in Jesus' footsteps
more earnestly in applying the gospel teachings to the
realms of healing, guidance and world affairs is, in the
words of Douglas Steere, their awareness that there is a
hair-line where prayer for things of this world can go
slithering off into magic, where man tries to control God
rather than laying himself at the feet of God and letting
God control him. Folks who have attended my camps and
read my books (not merely dipped into one or two of
them), realize that I draw that line very carefully. No
one should read this Part III until he has read both the
parts that preceded it. But when one really lays himself
at the feet of God he discovers that the truest thing Jesus
ever said was "Seek *first* the Kingdom of Heaven and its
righteousness, and all *these* things will be added unto
you," and what are these things but the things that pertain
to our daily life? The very core and center of the Lord's
prayer was "Thy Kingdom come . . . on *earth* as it is in
heaven," and the burden of Jesus' sermon on the Mount

and of all his parables was how to bring that heaven into manifestation in the affairs of our practical life.

The simplest way for you to bring heaven to earth is to see the footprints of heaven in the outer realm around you, transmute them through meditation and contemplation into your inner philosophy and hold them as the blueprints of God's perfect harmony in your deepest consciousness till God's blessing is breathed upon them, and then let them flow out again in faith and love and crystalize in lovely actions, beautiful creations, inspiring poems, miraculous healings and transformed lives.

PART III

Applications to the Problems of Life

CHAPTER XII

Friends

IN THE second dimension we deal with people on the level of our five senses. We see them, we hear them, we touch them, and in crowds we even smell them. As we grow more intimate with them, we rise into the third dimension where we shake hands with them, and say endearing words to them, and when they become a part of our own family, we even kiss them. The folks we would become better friends with we will go out of our way to meet; we will take pains to please them, we will entertain them, we make gifts to them.

If we would become a political or social leader where we would have to multiply our friends into thousands we find it helpful to study books on how to win friends and influence people; we enroll in courses of "charm," or take instructions in public speaking or salesmanship or character analysis or applied psychology. We even buy books on etiquette and try to learn all the rules that govern politeness, such as how to dress for proper occasions and which fork to use first at a banquet. These are some of the three-dimensional ways to win the good will of people.

This three dimensional level of man's relationship to man can run a wide gamut from the most superficial affection to the most devoted loyalty. On formal occasions one can easily shock the sensibilities of others by coming in street dress, and yet offend no one if he ends the banquet puffing at cigarettes or drinking evil-smelling alcohol. In a church the same behavior would offend all. Such are some of the strange, inconsistent customs of dealing with people in the third dimension.

Many have been the attempts to classify people. They have been classified according to race, to nationality, to religion, to sex, to political affiliation, or social rank, but Jesus Christ cut across all these superficial distinctions and partitioned mankind into three basic categories into which they fall in natural relationship with us.

The first group are those we feel naturally drawn to, the folks that God has selected from the beginning of time for our lives to be thrown with. The second group are those that neither by proximity, affinity, or other relationships do we find ourselves drawn to. The third group are those with whom we do business or meet in passing without any need of raising the question either/or.

The only thing we need to look out for he cautioned us, was never to let our behavior to these three groups descend to the second and first dimensional level, but at every opportunity that presented itself, to be prepared to lift it up to the fifth, sixth and seventh dimension. To this end he said, take heed that the affection you bear toward those you are drawn to doesn't descend into lust (even in your heart); and take heed that your lack of natural affinity to those you are not naturally drawn to doesn't descend into intolerance, disgust and hate (even in your heart); and finally, don't mistrust or cheat those with whom you do business.

But suppose the one you are drawn to gets an infatuation for you, someone asks, suppose he desires you to go a mile out of your way with him? Then Jesus tells us to go two miles, and the infatuation will either wear off or be turned into wholesome comradeship and good will. Suppose the one you are not drawn to slaps you on the cheek? Then lovingly and forgivingly turn the other cheek and he will become your friend for life. Finally, what if the one you do business with takes advantage of your willingness to trust him without contract or formal note? Suppose he steals your very shirt off your back? Then give him your overcoat as well and keep on trusting and he will make restitution for all he has stolen; or, if he fails to do so, what you have lost will return to you from some other source. If you follow these instructions, said Jesus, you cannot lose. Even where defeat seems to loom, you can turn defeat into victory.

Never was such an amazing code of conduct presented to mankind before. Thus Jesus revolutionized all our relationships with people in this three dimensional world of ours by opening the flood gates and letting all the powers of the higher dimensions flow in upon them and bless them.

When one enters the area of the fourth dimension, he goes beyond the third and second dimensions enslaved to the intellect and five senses, and finds himself in the field of extra-sensory perception. It was on this level that Jesus was speaking when he advised mankind not to lust in their hearts and not to hate in their hearts—revealing that the inner thought was as powerful as the outer action.

Luther Burbank was speaking on this level when he wrote that the time would come when people who threw out hate thoughts, envious thoughts and other negative thoughts into the atmosphere would be considered just as much enemies of society as people who threw poison into wells. There is no question at all why wide sweeping plagues always follow in the wake of great wars; it is because of the veritable flood of hate thoughts, fear thoughts and despair thoughts that thousand of people are throwing out upon the air. The flu followed World War I; infantile paralysis followed World War II.

One reason why movie stars find it so hard to live a normal family life is because so many million theater goers are falling passionately in love with them every night their faces appear on the screen. With such floods of emotional, lustful, possessive thoughts pouring in upon them, no wonder their so-called private lives are so often pulled out of balance. Indeed no group so desperately needs the loving protection and powerful guidance that can be found only on a still higher dimension than the performers in the moving picture industry.

On the other hand, a great and good man who is accepted by a large block of society as a saint finds this undergirding of faith in him a great impetus toward sainthood. There is no question whatever that Gandhi, who considered himself a very weak human being was literally hoisted into sainthood by millions of loyal disciples.

A woman who fears that her husband is becoming infatuated with other women can help redeem the situation by stepping into the fourth dimension and saying every night before she falls asleep, "Never forget, John, how dearly your wife, Mary, loves you and believes in you and wants your highest happiness." If she confines herself to this extra-sensory approach and refrains from all nagging, beseeching, arguing and quarreling, her chance of success will be much greater. I knew a man who won his sweetheart by saying every night, "Adelaide Emerson, Paul Anderson loves you."

A wonderful way to win or hold friends is to set aside a period each day merely to love them without possessiveness. A minister I know has a big cardboard on his desk with pictures of the friends he most cherishes pasted on it, and every once in a while he looks at them and loves them. This seemingly casual insignificant practice actually blesses, protects, and strengthens them in ways that cannot be measured. Moreover, in the fourth dimension of radiation and counter-radiation everything you send forth returns to you. For instance, Frank Laubach puts pictures of Jesus all around his room and as a result, not only Christ, but Christ-like people are drawn to him wherever he goes.

My son, Miles, upon starting his senior year in Central High School, St. Paul, realizing that he had been cold and aloof from his classmates, asked his mother every morning to pray that he would love everybody that day. To his own amazement he was not only elected president of the immense senior class but later was voted the most popular boy in the entire high school.

Wonderful are our opportunities for not only increasing our friendships but also for purifying and ennobling them by a proper use of this fourth dimensional extrasensory way of loving them.

On the fifth dimensional level we step into rhythm with our own Divine Plan, the pattern God has made for us in the Mount, and here we find safer, more solid foundations for building lifelong friendships than on any lower plane. It is very true that some friendships like that of Ruth and Naomi, and David and Jonathan, were decreed from the beginning of time. There is no doubt that some marriages are truly made in Heaven. Every one of us has some natural affinities whom we can trust with our inmost secrets, and whom we can think aloud with or even be silent with without giving offense.

"Asleep, awake, by night or day,
The friends I seek are seeking me.
No wind can drive my bark astray,
Nor change the tide of destiny."
("Waiting"—Burroughs)

Years ago I composed this psalm prayer which I have "prayed" off and on ever since: "I believe that God has selected those persons who are to belong to my plan, and that through proximity, mutual attraction or need, they and I are continually finding each other out. I believe in praying for ever-increasing capacity to love and serve them and for greater worthiness to be loved and served by them in return. I believe in sending out a prayer to the Father to draw to me those who are meant to help me and to be helped by me, in order to express my life together with them."

If you are very desirous of forming permanent, unbreakable friendships I would advise you each morning to step into this fifth dimension and pray, meditate and know that every person sent to you this day will be sent to you by God. Trust that you will meet exactly the persons you want to meet when they want to be with you. To find your friends on this level you don't need to travel or write in the third dimensional manner; you don't have to depend on affirmations and mental telepathy in the fourth dimensional way. All you need do is to KNOW that God has the perfect plan for you and rest back in perfect TRUST. Then act upon the Divine Guidance that comes to you, and go, unafraid, to the persons you feel drawn to, and accept without question people who come to you even though at first you may want to avoid their coming. Put yourself completely in God's hands and let Him arrange the pattern of your life, yes, depend upon Him to choose your friends, acquaintances, and close partners for you.

And now you are ready to step into the sixth dimension where you may have the privilege of experiencing the real orchestration of souls. You can function in this area with the greatest power after you have found some mutuals, affinities, yes, brothers of your very soul on the fifth dimensional level. When you have found them, you will be drawn to seek opportunities to sit in mountain-top experiences with them in the sixth dimension as often as the occasions permit. And yet there must be no possessiveness. Your mother love must not descend into smother love. You must share your friends on this level with all mankind.

Step out along the love bands that knit you together, dwelling not so much upon the charm of personality in each as much as you rest upon the blissful heavenly love and peace that unites you with them. In Book IV Chapter IV in *Water of Life* * where I describe the third level in Heaven, you will find a complete picture of this sixth dimensional orchestration. Chapter VI of the same book reveals the heavenly power that radiates from the orchestration of heavenly-anchored friends.

When you enter the seventh dimension of friendship, the highest blessings are yours. You are then abiding in the Father, and all your friendships take on a heavenly tone. As you love your friend, you are really loving the blessed Christ in your friend. Then loving your friend in this heavenly way, you learn at last what is meant by the love of God. "He that loveth not his brother whom he

* *Water of Life:* Glenn Clark—Macalester Park Pub. Co.

hath seen, how can he love God whom he hath not seen?"
(I John 4:20) At last you know the reality and the blessed
joy of loving the Lord thy God with all thy mind, all thy
heart, all thy strength, and all thy soul. From this time
on you are never lonely. You will always have a friend
in Jesus. This level when reached can purify and ennoble
friendship on all the other levels.

CHAPTER XIII

Health

HEALING on the third dimensional plane as practiced in the world today consists of applications of hot or cold water to the parts affected, of salves and ointments, of massage and adjustments of the bones and muscles; or the application internally of medicines and drugs and vitamins and the control of diet. The only way to penetrate to the inside organs themselves is by ultra violet rays of some kind or the incision of the surgeon's blade.

But when one steps up into the fourth dimension the organs are laid as bare and exposed to the eye of the soul as the outer body is exposed to the eyes of the physician. This can be illustrated by an analogy drawn from the second dimension. A two dimensional man is a flat man living in flatland, a land of only length and width and no height. When height is added he becomes three dimensional. A page from any physiology book will reveal the flat picture of a man with all his organs exposed. Let us imagine the other flat men who reside on this sheet of paper, coming together to consider what ails him and how they can pull the ailment out of him. But, alas, they cannot raise their hands or heads up into the air and look down upon the interior of this man, all they can do is to come to the outer boundary of his body and there stop.

If one of his organs is out of place all they can do is massage, or if need be cut into it from its outer boundary.

But any of us three dimensional creatures can look down upon these organs from above and from our superior height we can easily rearrange the parts exactly as they should be arranged. In exactly the same way people living, moving, and having their being in the fourth dimension can look inside three dimensional bodies and readjust the position, the form, and the very action of the organs which seem out of harmony with the rest. This can be done through the simple application of the newly discovered laws of psychosomatics; in other words, through the penetrating power of the emotions which do not stop at the outer surface of the body but vibrate deep into the secret parts from an entirely higher dimension.

An entire new breed of fourth dimensional doctors has been suddenly released upon mankind by this new discovery of an old truth enunciated thousands of years ago: "As a man thinketh in his heart, so is he." Learned books on psychosomatics are merely putting into big, unpronounceable scientific language what Jesus stated in simple terms two thousand years ago. "Not that which goeth into the mouth defileth a man, but that which cometh out of the mouth. This defileth the man" Matt 15:11

When I came to St. Paul in 1912 a woman on the next block was dying of cancer of the throat. She had been to all the greatest physicians in America and not a one gave her any hope. At last she went to a woman who believed in prayer.

"There must be someone you hate," she was told.

"There certainly is. I can't even think of her without feeling sick all over."

"Unless you forgive her I can't pray for you with any hope."

"I will never forgive her," she replied, and so they parted.

That evening when she told her husband he made no comment until they were ready for bed. Then he said,

"Let us kneel down together and have a prayer."

As they knelt he put his arm around her and said,

"Now we are not going to get up till you forgive that woman."

"Then we'll kneel here all night."

But before morning she relented and forgave the woman. That was in 1912. In 1947 I met her in Miami. She was in the front row of an audience I was addressing, the healthiest looking person in the room, almost as young looking as she was thirty-five years before.

Here was a definite example of how a changed emotion in the fourth dimension penetrated where it was not safe for a surgeon's knife to operate and changed cancer cells into healthy cells within a matter of days. A fourth dimensional doctor can reach into a man's throat and lungs and erase all asthma conditions by the simple method of washing out the emotions of self-pity. He can lower the blood pressure by sweeping out rebellious resentments, and relieve stomach ulcers by removing the sense of inadequacy. Elisha had a deeper wisdom than he has been given credit for when he commanded Naaman, the leper, to bathe seven times in the river Jordan. In my book *How to Find Health Through Prayer,* I state my faith that anyone who applies these seven baths to the whole of his being can be cured, no matter how long or how serious his illness. Try bathing your outer skin, your inner skin, your blood vessels, your lungs, your thoughts, your emotions, and finally your soul, and see whether any illness can stand before it. A regimen of bathing, drinking pure water, wholesome exercise, deep breathing, right thinking, happy emotions, and peace of soul is the combination par excellence for insuring sound health.

Thousands of chiropractors have joined the "Beamers" association, a group that has discovered that one-tenth of the adjustment for so-called illnesses is physical and nine-tenths spiritual. By getting on the beam and using "concept therapy" they have worked miracles comparable to the work of the psychosomatic M.D.'s. I explore this whole field in the book referred to above. Rebecca Beard, herself a licensed M.D., in her book *Everyman's Search;* Starr Daily in *Recovery* relating the healing experiences of Roland Brown, a Baptist minister; and Agnes Sanford, an Episcopal minister's wife, in *The Healing Light* all verify the points that I am making.

When we come to the fifth dimension we rise above the place where "work" is needed. We reach the place where man is visioned as he was originally made "after the likeness and image of God." Here man finds his divine plan with no manner of flaw. Anything wrong is merely an error in his or her thinking; or, what is a more accurate way of putting it, a twist in his feeling. The difference between the fourth and fifth dimension is that the fourth dimension physician observes the trouble and works hard mentally and spiritually at removing it, while the fifth dimensional physician calmly looks at the perfect pattern given man in the Mount and by refusing to see the wrong twists or errors, trusts that they will fade away. As the psychosomatic physician feels at home in the fourth dimension, the metaphysical physician feels at home in the fifth demension. Needless to say, it depends very largely upon which level the patient lives, which physician he should summon for help.

St. Paul was standing in the fifth dimension when he assured the sailors on the storm-ridden sea that no one would drown because an angel had let him look into the future and see his safe arrival at Rome. Rickenbacker had more than his share of hairbreadth escapes but always came through because of his innate fifth dimensional sense of a destiny controlling every event of his life.

When we reach the sixth dimension we step into the orchestration of harmony and contagious love, an orchestration which can use the penetrating rays of the fourth dimension or the steady visions of the divine plan of the fifth dimension, and with joy and serenity bring the finest and most permanent healing of all. It is fine and permanent because love is in it. When two or three come together in perfect harmony with deep love in their hearts for one another, that mutual love creates the perfect *wave-length* by which God's infinite healing *Love* can reach the patient. The only permanent healing power in the world is love and love can only find entrance into any situation through the path created by love. *For love is the power that draws all things into perfectly adjusted and harmonious relationship with everything else.*

Miracles can happen when a group of mutuals come together with love in their hearts for the patient, with absolute harmony and trust and love for each other, and rest in that love and trust until they rise into a sense of serene peace and exquisite ecstasy and actual bliss. And when such love is directed toward a so-called sick and ailing body, it draws every cell, nerve, gland, and organ in that body into perfectly adjusted and harmonious rela-

tionship with every other cell, nerve, gland, and organ.
Fix firmly in your mind this definition of love and it will
lift you into the sixth and seventh dimensions and you can
rest with absolute knowing that wherever love is released,
healing will take place. This exalted love, experienced on
the sixth dimension, is God Incarnate, for "God is Love";
and the moment we experience the Love of God, the door
opens wide for all the powers of the seventh dimension to
come into play.

Jesus taught us that higher than our own little efforts
to cast out wrong thoughts and bring in the right ones is
the Power of God when we turn to Him in absolute faith
and ask Him to set our inner house in order.

He can wash out all the sins and errors and mistakes
of the past. Indeed He has a cleansing fluid, the redemp-
tive love of Jesus, that is guaranteed to do what nothing
else can do. The greatest need of everybody in the world
is a blood transfusion of the love plasma that was shed
on Calvary. Christ can anoint the most hidden parts of
the inner body with Divine Love, the most powerful healing ointment in the universe.

But how can we invite this great Physician to take over
our case and expect His love to cause all our internal
organs to function in perfectly adjusted and harmonious
relationship one with another? The answer is simple but a
little hard to apply. We must turn to Him with a belief
that goes beyond belief, with a faith that goes beyond
faith—yes, where belief and faith merge into absolute
knowing. One purpose of this exploration of the higher
dimensions is to help turn our weak belief and our waver-
ing faith into complete *knowing*.

Christ's healing Love enters us when we turn to God
with remorse and repentance for our own sins and forgive-

ness for the sins committed against us. That is the first step and we have taken the second step when we turn to him with faith in his power to heal and gratitude for the blessings he has brought us in the past.

But in addition to these two steps—complete repentance and absolute faith—a third is very necessary—and that is that we relax our body, mind, and soul completely into His hands with perfect trust regardless of what the outcome is going to be. In other words to *let go and let God.* When you truly let go and let God take complete control you will be amazed at the results that will come to pass.*

---

* Those finding it hard to "let go" should send for Glenn Clark's correspondence course in Spiritual Therapy which guides the student through the "Seven Baths of Jordan." Payment optional with the student. Address Macalester Park Publishing Company, 1571 Grand Avenue, St. Paul 5, Minnesota.

CHAPTER XIV

Guidance

THE ART of guidance consists largely of learning which of life's limitations we must accept and which we can change. We have to accept our ancestors, our parents, and the age in which we were born. We cannot change our race or our sex. The radiant acceptance of these facts, these people, and this environment constitutes the first step in Guidance. Two-thirds or three-fourths of our Guidance is given to us on a silver platter without our having to do anything but accept it. Indeed the first virtue that is essential for the art of guidance is *obedience*.

The fact that we were born into a certain age means that we have work to do in that age. The fact that we were born into a certain nation means that we have some service we can render that nation. God has given us parents, brothers and sisters, and other human relationships, not by accident, but so that we can do something with or for those particular people.

The art of living consists of knowing what part of our so-called destiny we should accept and what part we have a right to change. There are some things about these walls of destiny that do not seem to be good, and that deep down in our heart we *want* to change. If a great desire comes to us deep down in our heart to change these walls, we should listen to it. If a change would hurt no human being, but bring blessings to all, you can listen to it as the Voice of God.

One cannot change one's sex, but Susan B. Anthony so yearned, deep in her heart, for the privileges that men had of sharing in the government, that the very fact that she was a woman who could not vote and yet yearned to vote, and had the gift of writing and speaking, opened the way and put her on the path of a creative life of reform that has brought blessings to many.

Dr. George Washington Carver could not change his black skin, and the possession of it often brought him into humiliating positions. But by using the native, almost primitive, psychic intuitions regarding nature and the growing things of nature, characteristic of his humble race, and adding to that the analytical mind and trained intellect obtained in northern universities where chiefly members of the white race attended, and crowning all of this with a great and simple faith that grew out of his habit of communing with God, he was able to map out for himself a destiny that transcended in many ways the destiny of men whose opportunities and racial backgrounds were more propitious than his.

Helen Keller seemed destined to go through life as a public charge, helplessly walled off from humanity by the three-fold limitations of deafness, dumbness, and blindness. One by one she overcame these. She learned to hear by placing her hands on the throat and lips of the speaker, and to speak by making her own throat act out syllables as theirs had acted. She even learned to tell color by the feel of the flower.

When Michelangelo went down to Rome one winter to work in sculpture, he found that all the Carrara marble had been taken by other sculptors. Only a large, broken, misshapen piece remained. With nothing else to work on he sat down in front of that unpromising piece of material and studied its possibilities and its limitations. Finally he figured out how, by creating a figure with arm outstretched in this way, and head bent that way, he could give a tolerable reproduction of David with his slingshot facing Goliath. He set patiently to work with the result that the choice room in the famous Pitti Art Gallery of Florence is given over entirely to this great masterpiece of Michelangelo's—the most prized object in that wonderful collection.

You are given certain possibilities and certain limitations. The art of living for you is to determine how you can create a masterpiece by actually utilizing your limitations, and by using to the fullest extent the talents God has given you. The difference between a pessimist and an optimist someone has said is that the pessimist sees a difficulty in every opportunity and an optimist sees an opportunity in every difficulty. Michelangelo, Helen Keller, and Dr. Carver were supreme optimists who created masterpieces out of seeming limitations. What a challenge that presents to us! What can we do with our life?

If man in his higher dimensions would make as great use of his gifts as the creatures in the lower dimensions make use of theirs, he would have no difficulty in living in accordance with the Divine Plan God has prepared for him. The acorn is obedient to its Divine Plan and grows into an oak tree. A bee flies in circles until it determines the direction of its hive, and then it goes on a "beeline" straight to that hive. The bee goes through space to its Divine Plan! The acorn goes through time to its Divine Plan. The question before us is, how can man, moving above time and space, find his Divine Plan with the same certainty as the bee and the oak?

Whales, I am told, always find their groups, salmon go back through the streams to their spawning grounds. Birds fly south in winter and north in summer; no one tells them how, they follow their Divine Plan.

Let us humble ourselves and go down into the second dimension for a while and see if we can catch the secrets of the birds and the beasts. Let us rest a while in our physical organism, so marvelously constructed of nerves and glands and deep subconscious urges, and see what it has to tell us. Take your cue from the squirrel. If you have the collecting instinct of this little rodent, direct your craving to a higher purpose and give it wholesome expression. Look at the beaver and if your practical hands itch to undertake constructive jobs, be true to your urge. Look up to the birds flying and soaring in the upper air, and if your imagination seeks these higher flights, try your hand at poetry and music and art.

Trust your body as a natural compass and barometer as sensitive as any instrument ever made by man. Navigators on planes know the secret of staying "on the beam." They pick up a signal from a city toward which they are flying and as long as they hold a beeline toward that goal, all is well. The moment they swerve seriously off the course either right or left, the jarring note on the erring side warns them.

The body that clothes our sensitive soul can furnish us signals for our guidance as effectively as these instruments of the air navigators if we only know how to interpret them.

Luther Burbank was so sensitive to the feeling of flowers and plants that when he went through a field to select

the special ones for further experimentation he chose
them so instinctively and so rapidly that he merely
dropped a white ribbon on each as he passed by and two
men following him tied the ribbons. Dr. Carver's whole
being was so attuned to the flowers that he could actually
talk to them and catch their messages in return.

When I came to St. Paul in 1912 I heard of the miracles of Indian Joe. If anyone were drowned in a Minnesota lake and no amount of dragging disclosed the body,
Indian Joe was summoned. He would demand that all
others leave the lake on the night he made his search.
Then seated alone in his canoe in the darkness, as uner-
ringly as a hound would follow a trail, he would be led
to the exact place where the body lay.

Starr Daily has told how men in the underworld upon
entering a city would sandpaper the palm of their hand
almost to the quick, then hold the hand high in the air
and *know* whether it would be safe to remain there or not.

Civilization has so neutralized the native instincts of
the body that the gifts of guidance on the second dimension are well nigh lost. But why not try it? For instance,
if every time you pick up the phone to make application
at a certain company, you get a headache, try another
company. If every time you telephone a man to make a
deal the line is busy, don't think it is a mere accident.
God is warning you. If every time you feel a grudge
against your boss you get stomach ulcers, quit feeling that
grudge. When Amelia Earhart's plane crashed it was
God's warning not to attempt the around-the-world flight
until more prayer preparation was made. Her husband
was a man of wealth and gladly had another plane built.
It, too, crashed. The Lord was now shouting at her. But
she procured another plane and was off on her fatal jour-

ney. I dare say most of my readers haven't the sensitivity of the animals. But if George Washington Carver were hearing what I am saying, or my part-Indian friend, Gene Estes, they would catch the impact of it at once!

Let us turn to the third dimension where the process is as follows: Think out the situation, collect the facts, weigh them, analyze them, and compare them looking into causes and effects. At last come to the best decision you can. Then sleep on it. The next day see if the decision is clear cut, logical, and what is most important of all, if it brings peace of mind.

If the logical approach does not make things clear or if it is a situation that baffles a logical conclusion, or if it does not bring peace of mind, the next step is to rise into the fourth dimension. Just as the dog, in the second dimension, puts himself in tune with the odor vibrations which abound in the airways, try putting yourself with equal faith in tune with the guidance vibrations which abound in the fourth dimension. Just *know* that these vibrations are here, and move with perfect abandon wherever the impulse leads you. Electrical power is generated by vibrations set in motion by the alternate current produced by negative and positive poles. Guidance vibrations are set in motion by another kind of polarization, the need on the one hand and the supply on the other.

As the dog is the pathfinder par excellence in his dimension, we can do nothing better than use him as the model to follow in our fourth dimension. The secret of his power consists of three things; he has a very sensitive nose, and he has no inhibitions, and no opinions. The soul of man is very sensitive to guidance, but this sensitivity is simply smothered under the weight of his inhibitions and opinions. After your intellect in the third dimension has gathered the facts and weighed the causes and effects leading to several projected solutions, then drop all your thinking and step into the fourth dimension and wait quietly, perfectly uninhibited and perfectly unopinionated, for a solution to come to you out of the ethers. In other words, know with absolute certainty that wherever there is a need there is also a solution for that need somewhere out there in space and if you can get quiet enough the need and the supply will ultimately find each other.

The first law of guidance in the fourth dimension is emptiness. The secret of the dog's gift of guidance springs from an empty mind. Socrates had that emptiness. His chief virtue was that "he knew that he knew nothing." This enabled his guardian angel to give him perfect guidance every morning. George Washington Carver had that emptiness. The little flower was "the conductor" that in the early hours brought him guidance out of the ethers for the whole day.

I find my emptiness in the pool of Siloam. Remember, it was perfectly still, except when an angel of the Lord came down and ruffled it. Then the *first one in* after that movement found the healing he sought. I quiet my mind. It becomes empty. No fear, no resentment, no inhibitions, no opinions of any kind, no wishful thinking; as cool as the pool of Siloam. I am lost in the Spirit. Then the first thought that comes to me, the first impression, the first urge, I accept as the angel of the Lord—and I act upon it. Ninety-nine times out of a hundred I find it is the right one.

But it is in the realm of the fifth dimension where guidance comes the most perfectly and with the least effort. Here, as you know, the perfect patterns reside. The finished plan awaiting you there is whole, perfect and complete. All you need do is tune in to it.

To see the pattern ahead in Time, all you need do is to climb to a high vantage point, just as you would when you would foresee what was ahead in Space, and from that vantage point, see exactly what obstacles you have to weave your way through, and what limitations you have the privilege of making a detour around. Here is an example of such a detour, which saved a life:

One Sunday morning I received a telephone call from Mrs. Simpson, one of my dearest friends in Minneapolis. She said, "Can I see you this morning regarding something that is of great importance to my life—it is something that cannot be put off, as I am leaving for the Mayo Hospital tomorrow."

I replied that I could see her after my morning Bible Class at Plymouth Church. But little was I prepared for the unusual story I was to hear.

"Last Wednesday morning," she began, "I received a telephone call from Miss Stella Holbrook, one of my friends. Her voice betrayed great excitement, and I could tell that she was under enormous strain. She said, 'My dearest friend is in deadly peril. I must see you immediately.'

"In a few moments she arrived at my apartment. She looked haggard and as she sat down she looked me searchingly in the face. 'The one who is in deadly peril,' she said, 'is yourself.'

" 'What!' I exclaimed. 'Why, I haven't been sick for years, and I never felt better in my life than I do at this moment.'

" 'No matter,' she said, 'you must see a doctor at once.'

" 'Explain yourself,' I said.

" 'You must listen to me, even if what I say may seem absurd. I had a dream about you last night. I could see you walking up and down the room holding your head between your hands. Finally you turned toward me and I could see that you had gone insane. It made such a deep impression upon me that I couldn't sleep. I walked the floor all night.'

" 'What!' I exclaimed. 'This sounds absurd!'

" 'No matter how it sounds,' she replied, 'you must see a doctor, if only for my own peace of mind. I never had a dream that was so real. Promise me that you will go to a physician at once.'

"So I promised and went. To my surprise the doctor discovered that I had a tumor that might press upon my brain and cause insanity unless something were done about it right away. He said that I should be operated on at once. I told him that I wanted to have Rochester check. So I am starting to Rochester tomorrow morning —but I wanted to talk with you before going and have your prayers joined with mine."

"To pray for a situation of this kind," I began, "and to pray with faith, requires that we first clear the ground. Anything associated with divination of any kind tends to make one feel helpless. How can one turn aside the hand of Fate? That fear is foolish—first of all we must understand that there is no power in the psychic realm—and that is the realm where divination resides—that can stand against the far greater power that functions in the spiritual or the heavenly realm. To foresee a thing in Time, is just like foreseeing a thing in Space. If you saw a washed-out bridge in front of you in Space, you would not run head-on into it, would you? You would make a detour around it. Well, it is the same way in Time. Miss Holbrook was able to climb the high hill of Love and see a bridge down, as it were, out there in Time. She foresaw an illness that you seemed to be running into head-on. But that will not be necessary. You can make a detour around it."

"And how can I do that?" she asked, just as naturally as she would ask the way to Des Moines. She was a remarkable woman, and I never saw greater poise and calm.

"Just as you would make a detour around a danger in Space," I replied. "Turn to the right. And by *right* I mean just exactly what Jesus meant when he said to Peter after he had been fishing all night without success. 'Cast out your net on the right side!' The right side is always God's side. In other words turn to God. Turn to Him completely and utterly, and put your entire problem into His hands with absolute faith that He has the power to remove the danger from you."

"I understand exactly," she replied. "You know that I have no fear for myself. I have never worried about myself, so you can count on me not to block your prayer in that way. Moreover, I can arrange my summer so that I can go off to the mountains and spend the entire summer in happy work and quiet prayer."

"Splendid," I replied. "Now I feel sure that God will take care of you."

Three months later I received another telephone call. "I am back from my summer vacation," came the voice, "and I want to invite you and Mrs. Clark to have dinner with me next Tuesday evening at the Women's Club."

On the veranda overlooking Loring Park, the most beautiful view one can obtain in the very heart of Minneapolis, Mrs. Clark and I sat down with her and with the majestic autumn sunset before us listened to her remarkable story.

"Well, I went to the Mayo Clinic," she began. "They

verified exactly what the doctor up here had said. The surgeon in charge advised immediate operation. But before taking me to the operating room he called in Dr. Will Mayo. 'Dr. Will Mayo,' he said, 'has something greater than the power of the average diagnostician. He has *intuition*—one might call it spiritual *insight*.' When Dr. Mayo examined me he verified what the other two doctors had already discovered, and then, as though speaking from a sixth sense, said, 'Don't operate right away. Go away for three months, and then come back, and we will decide what to do.'

"So I went away to the mountains. I spent the time literally and figuratively in the mountains of prayer. I had no fears, in fact I gave no thought whatever to this trouble, but turned my thought to God and my fellow man. Then when September came I went back to the hospital.

"When the specialist had finished his X-ray examination he exclaimed, 'Something must be wrong here. I must have Dr. Judd, the chief brain specialist, check up on this at once. What would people think of the Mayo Clinic if its records showed that you had a growth the size of a hen's egg in June, and that it had completely vanished by September!' So Dr. Judd examined me, and when he got through he seized both of my hands, jumped up and down and exclaimed, 'This is a miracle!' "

As one looks at the Divine Plan of this world, all arranged according to the pattern on the Mount in the fifth dimension, we can see how this world would today be an earthly paradise if our leaders would rise high enough to accept it from the God viewpoint, and not from the man viewpoint. Behold the Plan:

In God's Book of Life, in His Blueprint for this age,

we are ONE WORLD. The radio, the jet plane, the host of modern inventions drives that fact home to us. If we are one world we should become one people under one union of nations. We should have one central overall ruler. Do we all agree? And that overall ruler should be God. We should then unite in one great wish, one great prayer, and one great vote—that God become the One Ruler of this One World.

The moving pictures of this wonderful new scenario, entitled One World, are all prepared; they are in the cinema operator's machine, ready to cast their perfect pictures upon the screen. But who is going to operate the machine? Ah, there is the question. If some over-impatient operator runs it, using ultra-rapid motion, the picture will become a jumble, running together until nothing is clear. If he be a doubting operator, using ultra-slow motion, the pictures will move so slowly that intervals between eras of prosperity, instead of being lovely periods of transition, will be so drawn out that they will become horrible times of depression, unemployment, and suffering. If self-centered egotists turn it, they will turn the machine *backward,* letting scenes of harmony arranged by God be changed into scenes of discord, scenes of love into scenes of hate, scenes of peace into scenes of war. Isn't that EXACTLY what is happening today? If in the decade 1935–45 Roosevelt, Hitler, and Stalin had stepped aside and let God operate the machine, we should be seeing today a veritable heaven on earth. The chapter on Dynamic Symmetry in Statesmanship will discuss this further.

But how can one rise to a high enough vantage point to get this clear view of the future? First of all we should admit that there are some who are more greatly endowed with this gift of foresight than others. But all can find the safe detour if they will turn their eyes upon God each morning and see Him and His plan as clearly as they can. In other words, if you would see ahead in space you should first of all get your field glass in focus. At first you see nothing—it is all a blur. Then a simple twist of the instrument and there you are, the blur is gone. To get your spiritual field glass in focus to see ahead in time, first get your spiritual lens in focus by turning to God in thought.

I have often said that if I were a business man and got out of bed on the wrong side some morning I would get back into bed and phone my office that I would not come until the afternoon. If in the afternoon I still found myself getting out of bed on the wrong side I would postpone my important decisions until the next day. The crash of 1929 could have been avoided had all the business leaders of America had their field glasses trained in focus on God and the good of all instead of upon greedy profits each for himself.

The fifth dimension has no past and no future. All time comes to a focus in the Eternal *NOW*. Jesus stood in the fifth dimension when he said, "Take no anxious thought for the morrow, for the morrow will take thought for itself." The special key to opening the door to perfect guidance in this dimension is the great fundamental law, that if you would prepare for the future which you have not seen, your first step is to straighten out the past which you have seen.

When I shave I shave the face in the mirror. I have never seen my face. My friends have, but I haven't. I feel it but I have never seen it. All I see is the reflection in the mirror so I shave that, and when the job is completed I find that my face is shaved. By the simple process of removing the bristles of the past I remove the bristles of the future. If I look into the mirror with resentment I will see only resentment in the future. If I brood over the cheats of the past I will find cheats laying wait for me in the future. If I hang on to the hurts of the past I will bring hurts upon myself in the future.

Jesus was stating this law when he said, "Forgive us our trespasses as we forgive those who trespass against us." Shave away all the unforgiveness, all the fears, all the frustrations, and all the resentments of the past and a clear future will loom ahead. Have repentance for any wrong that you have done to others and make atonement if you can. If you can't make atonement to the one you've wronged, make it to someone else. If you find it hard to forgive yourself, avail yourself of the forgiving, cleansing power of the blood of Christ, and welcome the forgiveness of His grace to wash out all remaining "karma." Hard things in the past which you can't erase, accept with radiant acquiescence because they at least helped to turn you to God. Then train your lens upon the future and what a future you shall see! And how do you do that? Just refer to your Divine Plan and you will see your future coming to greet you.

We have spent a long time in the fifth dimension where the "blueprints" for most of our important guidance can be found. And now for confirmation of these plans move into the sixth dimension and gather your choice spiritual friends around you. Step into the silence around the pool of Siloam, and when the angel ruffles the water let the first one in give his impression. If the others agree with him, you can have confidence that the guidance is right. But here the key word is *agree*. It is the key that Jesus gave us in His mighty promise, "When two or three agree, anything they shall ask will be done for them of the Father." You must have absolute oneness in the group. Get still. Then when you drop all inhibitions, all opinions, all wishful thinking, and try to think only of God and of the love that binds you all together in harmony, your guidance can come clear and true. Put your problems in the form of a question—just one, and know that the answer resides in the question as the plant resides in the seed. Plant the question in loving soil and the answer may leap forth.

If the group is not harmonious enough or clear enough ask some close kindred soul to join you alone in prayer. Sometimes the best guidance of all comes through asking a child between four and seven, the age when he is least inhibited and least opinionated, and you will be amazed at the wisdom of his answer.

And now you are ready to enter into the seventh dimension, coming into the presence of God himself. He has been reaching you in all the lower dimensions—indeed most of us get his messages easiest when they are "stepped down" to us through a number of gradations,—in primer-size letters that can be read on the lower levels. But once in his presence all our needs can be solved.

On the seventh dimension one naturally turns to God's Holy Book. There we find him as our teacher, our partner, our guide, and the light upon our path. There we can lean back utterly upon the promises in his Holy Word. Psalm 32:8 gives us God as a *Teacher:* "I will instruct thee and teach thee in the way which thou shalt go." Proverbs 3:6 gives us God as a *Partner:* "In all thy ways acknowledge him and he shall direct thy paths." Then Isaiah 58:11 gives us God as our *Guide:* "And the Lord shall guide thee continually and satisfy thy soul in drought, and make fat thy bones; and thou shalt be like a watered garden, and like a spring of water, whose waters fail not." John 8:12 gives him as a *Light:* "I am the light of the world." Yes, he is a lamp unto our feet.

The key word in the seventh dimension is *Ease*. Let go and let God. Do things effortlessly, easily. Let your mind work conversationally; talk it over with God aloud, but quietly. Ask him to use your lips and talk to you. Or sit down and write your question and then when the Voice within speaks, write the answer that comes through naturally and easily.

Sometimes God uses our mind to bring us thoughts that we would not otherwise think, thoughts that intuitively tell us whether it would be foolish to go on, or to stay behind. Sometimes he uses our emotions, and when we are in tune with him we can accept it as guidance not to undertake a task when a great depression or abhorrence comes to us every time we consider taking it. If peace and happiness descend upon us every time we turn to another solution, we can accept that, too, as guidance. All these thoughts and all these different feelings should be listened to, as, other things being equal, they are the very Voice of God trying to get through to us.

When you ask the Lord for guidance and have a sense of peace you may know that God has planned it. There are fourteen places in the Bible that describe peace as the gift of God. When you get that peace, then you will know you have made the contact. Then you can know that all will be well.

CHAPTER XV

Inspiration

I HAVE often told my students that the power that runs all the machinery of the world is produced by falling water. No struggle, no effort, it just falls. But in order to fall it has first to surrender itself to the sun and be drawn up. The power that is created by the waterfalls comes from water that has been drawn up to a higher *altitude* level by the sun direct. The power created by the water in the average factory comes from water lifted through the combustion of coal or gas (in other words "canned" or "bottled" sunshine) to a higher *temperature* level in the boiler and as it descends to a lower temperature level in the generator, the power is produced.

The higher up the water is drawn, I told my students, the greater the power that is produced. In the same way, the higher you rise and the more effortlessly you go about your creative writing and speaking, the more powerful your message will be.

And then I proceed to cite the levels.

If you remain in the third dimension and write your theme from a sense of duty, your only object being to win an A or B grade, your theme will be a worthy contribution for the waste basket. If you can rise to the fourth dimension and get a real desire to write you may have something deserving attention. If you rise still higher and discover a vital, eternal truth awaiting you in the fifth dimension, you will at last have something worth while to write about. This discovery flowing down from this height will awaken your desire in the fourth dimension to bring it into the finest expression you know how in the third dimension.

But if you rise still higher, into the realm of love and harmony in the sixth dimension, and make that your starting point, you will find that through the perfect orchestration of the love and joy in this high fellowship, many vital and eternal truths will be born out of this blessed communion of souls. Finally, if you rise to the point where you can say, Lord, you take this pencil and write this message through my hand, the greatest inspiration of all will come to you.

And so I found that if I had my writing class begin with a period of silence wherein each in his own way mounted into the seventh dimension and made contact with the God of all life, and if I took pains to see that loyal love and good will prevailed among the members in the sixth dimension and if I helped stimulate them to find an eternal truth in the fifth dimension, the writing improved fifty percent.

One day, a student of mine, Marion Daily, who was to represent Macalester College in a national extemporaneous speaking contest where there were to be 100 contestants, came to me for advice. Instead of telling her how to gather material, how to organize it, how to express it—all valuable enough in the third dimension—I lifted her at once into the sixth dimension. "When you get up to speak,"

I said, "know that everybody there loves you. Look out upon them and love them all and make it your sole objective to make them all happy."

When she was fortunate enough to reach the finals and the subjects were drawn, two of the competing girls burst into tears. She cheered one successfully but the other said, "I drew a topic I don't know anything about." "I know a lot about that," said Marion, "let me help you outline your talk."

After spending half the hour helping others, she turned to prepare her own speech. When she came to speak, she gave no thought to winning the prize; she gave all her efforts to loving the people and making everybody happy. She succeeded so well in making the five judges happy that they gave her first prize.

And so my students discovered that any creative work done on the third dimension ended up in the waste basket, and not until they rose into the fourth dimension did they find themselves above the field of drudgery and in the realm where true art begins. Instead of three dimensional Dynamic Symmetry of *command* and reluctant *obedience* they had reached the fourth dimensional realm where the Dynamic Symmetry of earnest *desire* finds its balance in confident *relinquishment*. A successful sculptor gave a perfect illustration of this: "When I am given a commission from an owner of a large estate for a statue, I plant the desire to bring this forth in appropriateness and beauty in the back of my mind, and then I go off and leave it perhaps for weeks, giving no thought to it whatever; that is, no conscious thought. Then one day the owner of the estate calls me and asks how I am getting on. Then I stretch out under a tree with my head in the shade and my feet in the sun, and get very quiet to see what comes through.

And, sure enough, there gradually unfolds the perfect figure as I want it brought forth. Then I get my clay and start working with zeal and enthusiasm and keep working till the statue is done."

Indeed this alternation of desire and relinquishment, followed by the Dynamic Symmetry produced by the pendulum swing of *stillness* and *enthusiasm,* is the key to the skill of all natural born artists. When Wordsworth beheld a field of daffodils he planted the *desire* to record it in verse. He then *relinquished* it to do other things but deep down in his sub-conscious mind the desire abode awaiting its time:

> "For oft when on my couch I lie
> In vacant or in pensive mood,
> They flash upon that inward eye,
> Which is the bliss of solitude;
> And then my heart with pleasure fills
> And dances with the daffodils."

Then one day sitting in his garden following a period of deep quiet the poem would burst upon him almost in its entirety and with breathless enthusiasm he would put it upon paper to bring happiness to people for all time.

The pendulum swing on the fourth dimension is the perfect Dynamic Symmetry by which the perfect work of art all ready and waiting on the fifth dimension comes through. The Dynamic Symmetry on the fifth dimension can be summed up in the confident faith expressed through unhurried patience and peace of such men as Michelangelo, Rodin, and Borglum who claimed that all they had to do was to cut away the clay that didn't belong, the statue was already there.

When one rises to the sixth dimension the Dynamic Symmetry takes on the high voltage of an audience who loves the speaker, eager to hear his message, and a speaker who loves his audience, eager to fill their need. Such a combination releases more creative power than anything else under heaven itself.

Ruskin's mother's pride and interest in her son, in spite of all the "smother-love" attached to it, undoubtedly did more to bring forth his genius than all the professors at Oxford combined. The Brownings' poetry flowered in the light of their love. The covers of this book could not contain all the names of great men whose powers were brought to fruition through the warmth of another's deep interest and love. I have often explained how my own flow of books in these later years, at the rate of a book a year, was really drawn out by the loyal friends who attend my Plymouth Bible Class in winter and my Camps Farthest Out in the summer. Instead of being interruptions to the writings of my books, the class and the camps are the actual creators of my books.

Finally we come to the highest dimension to which man can rise—Union with the Father. Work produced on this level will never die. The reason why the Holy Scriptures have outlived all other literature is because the Hand of God was behind the men who wrote them. The Epics of Homer and Virgil have the mark of permanence because they opened with invocations to the Muses who were the guardians of the Holy Spirit in those days. The Book of Job and the book of Faust both have their opening scenes in heaven and both—one written in ancient, and the other in modern times—will live forever.

So I say to all who would create anything in this world, whether it be a speech or a happy home, rise up as high as you can and then fall effortlessly over the situation. The way to overcome any problem in life is to come up over it. Jesus puts this truth in matchless words, "Seek first the Kingdom of Heaven and its righteousness and all these things will be added unto you."

And what will you find in the Kingdom? Love! And what is Love? Here is the answer in the form of a prayer, the mere repetition of which will bring inspiration to anyone doing creative work:

Our Heavenly Father,
We know that Love is perfect understanding,
For Love is the light which makes all things clear,
For Love is the giving up of self to the Larger Self,
So that the Larger Self pours through us as through a channel,
And this activity of Love is perfect Wisdom, is perfect Understanding,
Bringing perfect Inspiration, perfect Peace, perfect Joy.
When the Larger Self speaks, all knowledge, past, present, and to come,
Speaks through us without check and without limit,
For that which is in part is passed away,
And that which is perfect is come.
For man, standing rooted in eternal Love, relaxed to its eternal har-
    monies,
Makes of himself a conch
Through which the music of the spheres finds voice and utterance,
And man, divested of self and expressing Thee,
Stands witness to Thine imperishable Glory.*

* The Soul's Sincere Desire, Glenn Clark, Little Brown & Co., Boston.

CHAPTER XVI

Finances

YOU WILL find nine-tenths of the people of the world who live in the third dimension expending most of their energy striving for better jobs, greater economic security, and more outstanding financial success. Toward this security and success they are using all kinds of techniques and marshalling all their mental and moral and physical attributes to achieve their ends.

"The secret of success is *industry,*" said Benjamin Franklin; "*frugality,*" said Calvin Coolidge; "*clever advertising,*" said Bruce Barton, and so it goes. When a business is "sick" an efficiency expert is brought in. He investigates to see if there is too large a payroll, or too many untrained or inefficient workers, or if they are using inferior materials, or are not catering to the right people. Books on how to win success in business are legion.

Our economic order on the third dimension can be likened unto an oil field filled with pumps. When oil is beneath the ground all we do is sink a shaft. But as one rides through the oil fields he sees something else besides the shaft, something that looks like a see-saw in constant rhythmic motion. That completes the picture. Make contact with the source and fall into harmonious balanced rhythmic action and the hidden riches become available for us.

Look at the fulcrum on which a teeter-totter is based. The fulcrum does not move no matter how much the children seated on the ends of the teeter-totter rise and fall. As a matter of fact, nothing is either gained or lost by this motion. As far as one end of the board goes up, the other goes down. The equilibrium is never really disturbed, but the children on the ends of the teeter-totter get a lot of fun out of it.

Let us put a bank, with its deposits of gold, in place of the fulcrum. Let the teeter-totter consist of a man coming to take money from the bank. But he really takes nothing; he does not break the equilibrium. He replaces every cent he takes out with an equal sum in the form of what is called "collateral." After many months he returns the money he borrowed and withdraws his collateral. Nothing has really happened to the fulcrum but in the meantime a hundred new homes have gone up.

So while nothing happens at the central fulcrum, the fact that the fulcrum existed, the very fact that it did nothing but remained itself, has in the first of these instances, led to making two children happy, and in the other to making many people happy.

When we step into the fourth dimension we don't have to locate any particular and definite source of wealth in the ground or in the bank. Just as Dynamic Symmetry in the material realm is demonstrated by negatively charged electrons and the correspondingly positively charged protons, each seeking and finding each other, so Dynamic Symmetry in the financial field is illustrated by the unfailing way in which our needs are met when we have put ourselves sufficiently "on the beam" to attract supply from sources we know not of.

When my sister, who lived in California, had two houses for sale and no buyers, I told her of this law and suggested that we pray, not for the sale of the houses, but that the persons wanting such homes, even though they might be 3,000 miles away would be made happy by the finding of them. The next day a friend of mine who lived three thousand miles away and who was considering moving to California asked if I could help him find a couple of cottages he could buy in that neighborhood. They were exactly what he wanted and both parties were made happy.

Another "pump" in the fourth dimension is a sincere desire and a humble relinquishment. The trouble with most of us is that we press down too hard on desire and fail completely on relinquishment. Desire is only one prong of Dynamic Symmetry. If we depended upon that alone, the world would get as out of balance as a teeter-totter with a child on only one end of it. Desire is the *Rhythm* end of this pumping process; relinquishment is the *Alignment* end. To want a thing very much and yet be willing to relinquish it if the Lord has some better plan, is the perfect attitude of mind to draw to you that which belongs to you.

When I desired an automobile for my wife and children to get out into the beautiful country on summer days but found I lacked the money to buy one, I recalled how my little girl had dug a well in the seashore sand and had waited patiently for the tides to come in and fill it for her. My wife and I laid our need for money before the Lord and told him that we felt sure that if it were a real "well" the tides of his supply could fill it for us, but if it were only an imaginary one, we would not expect his tides to fill it. In other words, we relinquished our seeming need entirely into his hands to decide whether it were real or not. This perfect balance of desire and relinquishment released the power that drew the *exact* sum we needed within the next ten days.

When we step into the fifth dimension we reach the place where all that belongs to us is already prepared and waiting. All we need do is produce our credentials and claim it. Anything that brings you happiness and peace, and hurts no one else, belongs to you. Nuts were made for squirrels. They have a perfect right to gather them. A dog or rabbit would be entirely out of his territory claiming nuts. The Lord allocates his gifts to those they actually belong to, and his distribution is guided and directed by the peace in the hearts of those to whom they belong.

The conventional way of drawing your own to you is to tithe. The surest way to draw to you that which is yours is to take steps towards giving others that which is theirs. Giving unto God that which is his opens the door for him to give you that which is yours. The Hebrew people were the ones who started tithing and became in their day the richest race in the world. The Mormon Church followed suit and has become the most opulent church of modern times. No member of the Mormon community has ever had to go on relief. They claim that every Mormon who has tithed willingly has prospered. Silent Unity, the Prayer Center of the Unity School of Christianity, receives thousands of calls for prayer every day, and they report that never has a tither asked for prayer for supply.

Matthias Baldwin, founder of the great locomotive works, made it his practice to set aside one-tenth of the earnings of the company to be used for religious and educational purposes. At one time his firm was encountering tremendous financial difficulties. He had no funds left to tithe with, so he made out notes signed by himself, which he later redeemed, all of which were paid. During this crisis his associates asked him to stop his practice of tithing, but he cried, "Why, that is my one safe investment."

A man who tithes said to me one day, "You can beat the bank of Monte Carlo once in a while but you can never beat the bank of God and his law. As ye give ye shall receive. It gives forth of its riches only to those who obey the law."

Another way of expressing the Dynamic Symmetry of the fifth dimension is the Spirit of Opulence balanced by the Spirit of Service. This is the teeter-totter that "pumps" wealth to people faster than anything else. Gold seems to be drawn to some people as iron is drawn to a magnet. These people love money and all the lovely things money can buy, but they also love to bless and help others with their money and let it serve others in every way they can. Love of money alone can close the door against its coming unless your other door is open for giving it forth to bless others; and he who gives lavishly without due appreciation of the value of what he gives is likely to die a pauper.

If I picked out any particular company that illustrated this combination I could think of no better one than International Business Machines, and no clearer statement of it than the credo of Thomas J. Watson: "We must give more than we get. I always get much more than I give. That is because I can give only what is within me, one single man, whereas I can receive what all other men have to give. All of our dealings with men must be mutually beneficial. They must be balanced. Both sides of a transaction must give happiness, not just one side. If you think you have the best of a deal with any man go think it over. If you conclude that he has not benefited equally with you then you have surely gotten the worst of the deal. If, in my dealings with men I lose money that is nothing; but if I gain money and lose a friend then I have lost heavily and I will run fast to catch his friendship and bring it back. If you hurt anyone you hurt everyone, therefore, if you help anyone you help uplift the whole human race."

On pages 228–231 of my autobiography, *A Man's Reach,* I give two striking examples of the working of this law. My booklet, *The Secret Power in Business,* has many more. Here are a few additional ones:

One day a man came into my office. "I am putting all my fortune," he said, "into constructing a factory to develop a new invention but the patents have been delayed in coming through. Now, just when we are ready to go into production we find another company has stolen our secret and secured the patents before me. I stand to lose all."

"The invention belongs to you?" I asked.

"Yes, but I don't know what a court of law will do."

"Remember this," I continued, "your own cannot be taken from you. I am going to ask you to memorize the first, third and last stanzas of John Burroughs' 'My Own Shall Come to Me.' Hold fast to that truth and I can pray for you with power."

Within a year his problem was solved and the sole rights for marketing this product in America and Europe were granted to him.

One day a college student came into my room. "Your philosophy didn't work last night, Professor. I was held

up by a highwayman and my watch was taken from me."
So, my philosophy didn't work? Well, that was just too
bad. But I knew Jesus' philosophy would work. I had
told this chap to have no fear—nothing that really be-
longed to him could ever be taken from him. A week
later he came into my room and sank back into a chair.

"I think I should tell you something, Prof. My father
three years ago found that watch in the back seat of a
taxi. He brought it home and instead of advertising it in
the Lost and Found column of the St. Paul paper, he
finally listed it in a little paper of South St. Paul seen by
no one but a few cattle men. So I guess the watch didn't
really belong to me."

So Jesus' philosophy worked after all, which reminds
me to give my readers this caution: if any of you are holding anything, from watches to real estate, that doesn't
honestly belong to you, you had better lock your house
very carefully every night, and keep all your contracts in
burglar-proof safes. If all you possess is what you have
honestly earned and truly deserve, you can leave your
doors unlocked and keep your valuable papers in your
business desk.

When we step into the sixth dimension we are where
orchestration of love and harmony and good will abound.
In that atmosphere any company that has a worthy product will succeed. Let me illustrate:

My father was manager of three companies, one after
the other. The first thing he did in each case was to invite
in the agents from all over the state and tell them, "We
plan to be one well related family, and we want, above
everything else, to share with each other a spirit of good
will and harmony." In each case the agents went out and
in one year doubled the business of the company.

I happen to know that the same spirit was created in his companies by my friend, Ralph Budd, as president, first of the Great Northern and later of the Burlington. He trained more railroad presidents than any man who ever lived, one of whom was his own son, John. All of them caught this gift of putting harmony and team work into everything they did. One of them who was a close friend of mine, Al Williams, was president in succession of Western Indiana Railroad, Lehigh Railroad, Western Union Telegraph Company and Westinghouse Air Brake Company, and into all of these companies brought the same spirit of harmony with the same outstanding success.

This law of Dynamic Symmetry on the sixth dimension has been put into words in a remarkable way again in the credo of Thomas J. Watson, "In all the seventy-nine countries where this business operates, we are all one brotherhood. We have but one thought, one creed—mutual helpfulness to each other. We feel that brotherhood in our very handshake. It is real. Our very language is a universal one. We all understand each other, no matter what our tongue. We want that friendliness to reach out into every other business. This business is a mountain of good thoughts piled one upon the other. If they are all good thoughts, our business will endure forever."

When we enter the seventh dimension we are in the presence of God. Many business houses would not feel at home in this rarefied atmosphere. But those that do have the seeds of permanence in them.

Arthur Nash took the Lord as his Senior Partner and his business prospered. Le Torneau took the Lord as his major partner so completely that he keeps only a tithe for his personal expenses and gives the nine-tenths to the Lord's work. Marshall Field never advertised in the Sunday papers and his business outgrew all the other businesses of its kind in the world. George Dayton of Minneapolis decided against advertising in the Sunday papers and his department store grew from the smallest to the greatest in the Northwest. J. C. Penney, Vash Young and scores of others I can name were outstanding examples of men who put God first. George Muller started his orphanages with no money but with such implicit faith in Jesus' promise that what one asks in the inner room with the door closed will come to him openly, that he never requested a penny from any man, and his prayers to God offered in secret brought seven million dollars. No wonder the Bristol Orphanages became the greatest in the world.

Once my friend, Harvey Hill, came to me with one of the most audacious proposals I ever heard.

"Americans don't know how popular religion can be made if people are offered the very best. In Winnipeg where I have often been they have the daring to rent an immense hall and bring the greatest spiritual leaders from all over the country, sell tickets and after a week of packed meetings they pay all expenses and have a sum to give the City Council of Churches besides. If you will choose seven praying people to undergird me with prayer, I will undertake to put on a Crusade for Christ such as Minneapolis has never seen."

"Do you have any money in case you fail?" I asked.

"Not a cent. Only my faith in God."

I tried to dissuade him from it, but he went straight ahead with a program that would entail the expenditure of $3,000. I did, however, gather seven God-inspired souls to meet with me once a week in prayer for God to bless the mission.

My premonition that Americans will gladly buy season

tickets for football but not for religion turned out to be sound. The only time the 2,000 seats were all sold was the night George Washington Carver spoke. When the Crusade was over there was a $1,200 debt. I called my prayer group together.

"We are a prayer committee and under no responsibility to undergird this crusade with money. But I have found the one point where religious leaders can hurt the cause of religion seriously is by lack of integrity about money. I suggest that we seven take some steps to wipe out this debt right now. I for one will gladly subscribe $300 from my professor's salary, and as the Koronis Camp Farthest Out has over $300 balance from last summer, I shall ask the treasurer to give $250 of that to this cause."

Immediately George Wheaton, the hardware man, said, "I will give $100," and C. H. Andrews, the grain man, said, "I will give $100," and Stella Wood, director of Miss Wood's School, said, "I will give $100," and in ten minutes the entire sum was raised.

I left the meeting and went to the college just as Mr. Frederick Bigelow, president of the Board of Trustees, was coming out. Professor Hall, the registrar, remarked as I entered the door, "Mr. Bigelow just now said that he never had a happier time in the world than the past hour sitting in that chair signing his name."

In my postoffice box I saw a colored slip of paper. A check for $300, a personal gift from Mr. Bigelow. I glanced at the boxes of the other fifty teachers. A slip in every box! How could Mr. Bigelow do it? Why did he do it? Did my gift act as a vortex to draw all these gifts from him? If it did, just think of the vast prosperity his gifts in turn would bring to him!

That evening a lawyer friend of mine called on me.

"My aunt, Mrs. Pomroy, will not be at the camp this coming summer. She is on her death-bed. But you know how full of outgiving joy she is. Well, she wants to have the fun of giving away her money before she dies. So she sends this check for $250 for the Camp Farthest Out."—I gasped. Exactly the sum I had promised to give from the Camp! "And this other check for $250 she wants to give to your Plymouth Bible Class."

As I went to my Bible Class the following Sunday my heart was full. I was walking in the Kingdom of Heaven. Yes, I was truly experiencing the Seventh Dimension. At the door of the class Mr. Wheaton met me.

"Something strange happened this week," he said. "A lawyer came to me from New York. 'I make my living finding lost money,' he told me. 'The receiver pays me half. Did you know you have $100 in the Citizens Bank?' I told him I never deposited a cent there in my life. He said, 'Come and see.' The cashier looked through his books and said, 'You have $100 deposited here 35 years ago.' I wouldn't believe it. He explained that it was originally in the American Bank. I told him I had deposited my savings as a paper boy in that bank long ago. 'But,' I said, 'it failed!' 'No,' he replied, 'it didn't fail. Our bank absorbed it!'" He handed Mr. Wheaton a check for fifty dollars and at his request the other half to the lawyer and whispered to him to return after seeing the lawyer off. When he returned the cashier was writing out another check for $83.00. "This is the interest," he said.

A woman so long indebted to Stella Wood that she had written it off her books brought her $100, and Mr. Andrews story would take a chapter in itself. His "returns" ran up in the thousands.

Things like this don't happen every day. Why did it happen in this case?

I think it was because everything pertaining to this Crusade was in the seventh dimension. A Crusade for Christ, a committee of unseen folks in an inner room, the shouldering of a debt to help a cause outside the givers—a daring attempt to bring the Spirit of Christ to a great city—and a clear cut case where the giving was without any expectation of reward. We let go of our money—not as an investment but as an adventure with God. Our act of unselfishness, without expectation of reward of any kind, to a cause the sole object of which was to bring folks to God, stepped us right into the treasure hold of God Himself. As fast as we poured out, God poured in.

There are few adventures that bring such joy to the giver. Try it and feel the bliss of union with your Master.

When we rise into the seventh dimension and accept our place as a Son of God we find we are surrounded by great riches. Then we discover that all the fruits and sweets the world has ever grown or man has made for man to eat are ours, and all the money ever minted, and all the pictures ever painted, and all the books ever written.

"Show me your fruits," someone may say. "Show me your money, show me your pictures, show me your books." Ah, friend, a million servants are taking care of these fruits and books and pictures for us. We would not want to be weighted down by the care of them. As fast as we need them, in perfect order and in perfect sequence, according to our needs, they come to us. A thousand men are digging gold out of the hills, other thousands are minting the gold for us. Bankers are taking care of it for us, taking care of it and giving it out to people who need it to pay us in exchange for services we may render them from time to time. The order and sequence that God has arranged for this money to come to us is according to the measure of service we render. Sometimes the money does not come in as large a measure as the service we render. Then we rejoice and are exceeding glad, for we know that we are having treasure stored up for us in Heaven, where "neither moth nor rust doth corrupt and where thieves do not break through and steal." Sometimes it comes faster and in greater measure than the service we render. Then we are humble and pray that our greed shall not disarrange the perfect schedule of the Master Planner and lead us to miss some of His beautiful scenery and some of His happiness and perfect joy.

But if we trust all to God and stay our mind wholly on Him, then all things come to us in perfect order and in perfect sequence, and our mind is kept in perfect peace, because we trust in Him. Then the world becomes one vast home where all are our brothers and sisters, and our loving Father watches over us carefully to see that all our needs are filled.

CHAPTER XVII

Statesmanship

THE HISTORY of the world has been for the most part a history of war. The art of statescraft has been largely an art of warcraft. The philosophy of nations has perverted the slogan "the survival of the fittest" to mean the survival of the best fighters—those who are the most adept in destroying the lives of others.

But every field of history contradicts the wisdom of this. Just as the dinosaur, saber-toothed tiger and cave bear have become extinct, and the gorillas, grizzly bears, lions and tigers are being supplanted by helpless cattle and sheep, so the nations who waxed great through the wielding of swords and spears are being replaced by nations who cooperate and serve. What were the conquering nations in ancient times? Egypt, Assyria and Babylon. What do they amount to now, and where are the mighty Medes and Persians? Who trembles today before the tramp of Macedonian phalanx "and the march of the Roman Legions"? Spain no longer dominates "the Spanish Main," and Britain is no longer "mistress of the seas."

The great armies of Napoleon under the mightiest general that ever lived succeeded in only one thing—bringing France into a period of decadence from which she has never emerged. Half a million magnificent men, tall and strong, marched with Napoleon to Moscow and only twenty thousand came back. The French race today is two inches shorter than one hundred and fifty years ago.

The only "fighting nations" that survive are Britain and Germany, and one is a shambles and the other a soft target for any atomic bomb that comes its way. Hitler has done for Germany what Napoleon did for France.

The United States of Soviet Russia and the United States of America have survived as the strongest fighting nations today because they have rarely used their fighting strength except in self defense. But unless these two nations now rise above the jungle methods of imposing their ideologies upon the world, their lights, too, will go out. The survival of the fittest is still the slogan the nations live by, but it will remain a snare and a delusion leading them to destruction unless the word fittest is properly redefined, not as the *fighters,* but the *lovers,* not those who *combat* but those who *cooperate,* not the *proud* but the *meek.* Jesus gave the best formula for survival ever given when he said, "The meek shall inherit the earth."

Which will be the great nations one hundred years from now? It doesn't take a prophet of the fourth dimension, or a seer of the fifth, or a sage of the sixth, or a saint of the seventh to prophesy that they will be China and India, the two meekest and mildest nations of the past— conquered, trampled on and dismembered by all the powers that did business with them. They will not conquer the earth, mind you, but inherit it; like a ripe plum it will fall gently into their laps after all the fighting ends and the shouting dies away. Whether the United States survives among the leaders depends upon two things: Can we be meek enough? Can we serve enough?

When we rise from the second dimension of war, where

America has always given a good account of herself, to the third dimension of diplomacy, our government has been revealed as a comparative novice at that game. At Yalta and Potsdam and practically everywhere we pitted wits against better equipped foes.

What the United States needs right now is a Board of Strategy that can match the strategy that Russia has been using against us. She has been out-maneuvering us on every level.

For one hundred years, Great Britain was a dominant power in the world. She perfected a strategy that has never been equalled before or since, until now Russia is using it with remarkable skill. The secret of Britain's strategy was to keep the two powers that were next to her in strength in constant antagonism or conflict with each other, while she rode safely on the crest of the wave.

Today Russia is afraid of only two nations: one is the United States and the other is China. Due to China's racial background, totally different from Russia's, and her centuries under the Confucian social system rooted in the family and totally opposed to Marxian collectivism, and the strategic location as the leader of all of Asia, Russia has more actual grounds for fear against China than she has against us. In short, due to her location and her resources, and her needs, China is in most respects a natural rival of Russia and a natural ally of the United States. If we ever got together, Russian strategy would fail. Her game is to play us off against each other and that she has cleverly proceeded to do. Through Machiavellian tactics Russia got us involved with China in a war which neither of us, left to ourselves, would have chosen. As two friendly Kilkenny cats, when their tails are tied together over a wire, claw until only a strip of fur remains, so all Russia had to do was to tie China and the United States together over the line known as the 38th parallel and then sit by and watch the "fun."

Long ago our War Department deduced from the experience of the western "gun-toters," that the nation which can get the draw upon its opponent has half won the war. This explains our elaborate organized attempts to "read the mind" of the enemy: first in the field of espionage; second, through air reconnaissance; and third, through radar. But we have not yet explored the fourth method: mental telepathy. Since Duke University has conclusively proved that telepathy exists, why cannot our government gather a few persons who possess this gift in an especially high degree and use them as the King of Israel used Elisha who informed him of every ambush the foe prepared for his troops before his men fell into their traps?

Let me illustrate how the debacle of Pearl Harbor might have been prevented: A few days after the Japanese attack on Pearl Harbor, December 7, 1941, which occurred at dawn, Hawaii time, but a little after high noon midwestern time, a woman, highly respected and very prominent in her little Minnesota town, called upon me in St. Paul.

"I am suffering under a guilt consciousness, a terrible sense of remorse over an amazing experience that came to me on Sunday morning, the 7th of December. When I awoke a voice out of the ether spoke distinctly to me, 'Wire the White House and cable Honolulu that Hawaii is in imminent danger!' I had never had an experience like that and the whole thing confused me greatly. Was it an authentic warning or was there something queer about *me?* I didn't want people to think me a crack-pot.

As the morning wore on it gave me no rest. At ten o'clock I felt I *must* consult someone I could trust, and I thought of you as one who might interpret what this meant. Then I remembered you had a Bible Class at ten and would probably be in church at eleven. I waited till twelve. Suddenly at noon the same voice came again, 'Too late to wire the White House. Cable Honolulu danger is at hand.' It seemed so absurd for little me to cable a message like this clear to Honolulu, so I remained in this state of confusion and inaction until, a little after one I turned on the radio, and the room was suddenly filled with the excited voice of some unknown announcer screaming to the world the terrible things taking place that very hour at Pearl Harbor. Do you think this disaster could have been averted had I acted on that first warning in time? Please, please, tell me, Dr. Clark."

Her anguish was pitiable. But I was able to bring a measure of peace to her when I assured her that human understanding at this time is so adolescent, if not actually infantile, along these lines, that any cables or telegrams she might have sent would in nine chances out of ten, have been cast into a wastebasket as the ravings of a crack-brained fanatic.

Eight years later my conclusion was verified when I visited Hawaii and discovered how even a more conventional warning of danger had been spurned by those in charge. A private soldier who was an amateur radio enthusiast kept phoning the army radio office, which had ceased operating for the night, that he was catching sounds of alien planes approaching. To every call he sent, he received the same answer, "Go sleep off your drunk." What would they have done to such a starry-eyed cablegram as this lady would have sent them? Isn't it time we began to throw other things into the waste-basket besides messages from heaven?

There are some thinking folk who believe that before the Pearl Harbor attack the Japanese Board of Strategy engaged a team of Buddhist priests especially skilled in Yogi technique of the fourth dimension to concentrate "black magic" or hypnotic powers upon the American Intelligence Department in Hawaii so powerfully as to numb them against detecting signs of the coming attack.

Greater protection than the telepathic vibrations of the fourth dimension, however, would be the clairvoyant gifts of actual divination of coming events long before their occurrence. This belongs to the field of the fifth dimension. As a matter of fact all the prophets of Israel who followed Elisha foresaw, through their fifth dimensional lens, doom and captivity coming upon Israel unless their nation stepped up into the sixth dimension and ceased their exploitation of the poor. As the nation failed to heed their warning it ran head-on into the ruin prophesied for it. Today the prophecy of doom is the same and today the nations are taking no more heed than Israel did of old. They are taking no steps into the higher dimensions as commanded. The more frightened the free enterprise countries get, the more frantically they concentrate on lower dimensions and the less on higher. Meanwhile the Russians have perfected a technique of forging poverty and insecurity into a weapon of aggression wherever they please. That seems to be the only weapon they need to wield to create war on any front where human misery opens the way. The nations where forms of cooperative effort have been adopted—Britain, Sweden, Norway, and Denmark—permitting emphasis upon production for use more than production for profit, are the *only* European nations that have no danger of communism within their own borders today. In contrast to these, Italy, Greece, and France, where the masses are exploited, can be taken by Stalin over the telephone. The same is true of the under-privileged nations of Asia. Most of the billions of dollars the United States has sent to Europe has been spent on arms and most of the remainder has fallen into the hands of the "haves" instead of the "have-nots." When I went to Europe in 1948 I found that was especially true in Greece, Italy and France.

A committee our government sent to the Philippines reports the islands are hot-beds of exploitation and graft. Neither the Philippine government nor ours is doing anything about it. The same was the case in Nationalist China. Some say the Rhee government in Korea was not too good. Certainly it is true of Indonesia and Indo-China. We are a Christian nation, and yet in facing these and other major crisis in the past fifty years we have not once used the Christ method to meet them. Gandhi, seeing our apostasy, chose to remain outside a religion which had so little faith in its Founder's teaching; instead he chose to follow the Founder without taking His name:

"Here was a man (Gandhi)," writes E. Stanley Jones, "in loincloth and with a lathee (bamboo stick) going out to do battle with the greatest empire that ever existed and promising not to return until independence had been gained. Never were two sides more unequally matched. But here was something more than a little man and a stick. Here was the embodiment of an idea; he would match his capacity to suffer against the other's capacity to inflict the suffering, his soul-force against physical force; he would not hate but he would not obey, and he would wear down all resistance by an infinite capacity to take it. Here was a technique that had been applied here and there in history, but never applied to a problem on the scale of nothing less than the freedom of one-fifth of the human race. The stakes were immense, and the cards seemed all stacked against him. How could he win? But we soon began to see the immense power of an embodied idea. The British were baffled. This was illustrated to me when a burly Irish military officer said to me: 'If only they'd fight with weapons we'd understand, we would show them something, but this. . . .' " *

Within this year I am writing, a movement started in Italy gives us hope that even the Christian nations may some day start applying the paradoxes of Jesus of the seventh dimension in the affairs of practical life. Indeed it is called the "upside down strike." *Between the Lines* describes it as follows:

"It began when 120,000 impoverished peasants had unsuccessfully petitioned their wealthy landlord, who owned 60 square miles of rich farm lands, for higher wages. Instead of a stop-work strike the peasant leaders finally persuaded their associates to double their efforts, do much more work each day than was asked of them, extend their activities to road mending, fence repairing, restoration of old buildings, etc., a veritable onslaught of voluntary services and good works! All would see how eager the workers were to help their employer increase his wealth if he would be just and generous with them. He would have to yield in self defense! What a stupid fool and scoundrel he would be not to reward and capitalize upon such good helpers!

"The idea has also threatened to spread to some Italian *industries*— workers at the bench voluntarily putting in extra hours working through holidays, devising ways to increase production, going all over the factory to rebuild, restore, improve the property; to support their request for a raise. A picket line can be pilloried by strike-breakers, supported by sound trucks blaring out anti-union epithets; armed guards can drive strikers from the plant; even the militia can be called out. But with this new idea, what on earth could a boss do?

"Let us suppose that this principle were applied to the international scene; instead of all the invectives we are hurling at the Chinese communists, a great campaign might be organized to send great quantities of surplus food, clothing, medicine, to hungry destitute China. We could accompany these shipments with an overwhelming publicity campaign so

* Gandhi, an Interpretation, E Stanley Jones, Harpers

all of China would know what we were doing. That is important, for then the Chinese communist leaders would not dare refuse our gifts for fear of a general revolt among the desperate Chinese masses—a revolt that would surely be forthcoming. Such a maneuver on our part would put a powerful squeeze on Russia's pretended friendship for China which had occasioned more of looting than of giving. The blow to Russia's prestige would be staggering.

"Then suppose, just as the Moscow politburo began to dig out from under the diplomatic impasse created by our moves in China and Europe, we should launch a similar 'upside down attack' against Russia! For the Soviet has not yet recovered from the war's destruction.

"All political scientists and historians would concede that such an effort would be the most devastating onslaught the Red Moscow tyranny has ever faced. There is not a diplomat who would not agree. Such an effort would change the face of the entire world outlook.

"But it would take something that our very rich country and its leaders so far apparently do not possess—a resource of hearts and mind and a creativeness and daring of intellect that our continued absorption in militarism does not permit."

It doesn't require a prophet of the fifth dimension to foresee what practically all the missionaries of Asia, from Frank Laubach and Stanley Jones down, have been proclaiming for the past twenty years, that unless the white races bring to an end their imperialistic exploitations of the dark races we shall be involved in a war in comparison with which World War II would appear a mere parlor game. But, as in the days of Jeremiah and Amos, the rulers listened to their war chiefs and disregarded their prophets. Instead of sowing love and reaping love, we sowed the wind and are reaping the whirlwind.

If the Christian Church had honestly accepted this forecast they would have started praying. If the political and economic leaders had accepted it and taken warning they would have ceased their exploitations of the dark races and instead established co-operative relationships for the benefit of all. As a result there would have been no war. Our governments by raising a billion dollars and sending missionaries, agriculturists, doctors and teachers to Asia, would have saved the expenditure of four hundred billions on war. Our churches, by training and sending one hundred thousand missionaries to carry the gospel of love, would have saved the world the need of giving fifty million of its young men in death.

Historical analysts report that America has never lost a war but she has never won a peace. It isn't surprising. We have a Department of War. When "finis" is written on the period of war—what then? We haven't a Department of Peace! This makes it clear to all lovers of peace that if we want war to end, the next step for our government to take is to establish a Department of Peace. The duties of such a department would be, first, to build a national foreign policy based on justice, friendliness and good will; and second, in case of war to plan in advance and put into effect a peace that would be fair, equable and lasting.

Knowing the long period of time that would be required to persuade a sufficient number of our law makers to bring about such an innovation in our national government and knowing that one act is worth a thousand words when the act is in accord with the will of God, a group of us have decided to set up a model Department of Peace and in a small way let the world see what a power such an instrument can be for good.

A hundred years before the Tennessee Valley Authority was established and the great work undertaken that carried prosperity to the citizens of many states, Colonel Lay of Birmingham, Alabama, got a conception of the wealth that could be brought to his native state if its water power, then going to waste, could be properly harnessed by the building of an immense dam. He spent a quarter of a century lobbying with the Government officials in Washington without avail, and only near the end of his life did he think of turning to private capital to bring his dream to pass.

With wars and rumors of wars impending all around us we cannot afford to wait a quarter of a century to have our dream come true. So without waiting for a reluctant Congress to act upon this suggestion, a great gathering of people meeting in Washington with Frank Laubach and me decided to profit by the experience of Colonel Lay and try to enlist the private capital of interested individuals (not the capital that is stored in banks but the capital that is stored in human hearts) and establish a Department of Peace right away.

In three large congregations in Washington in the opening days of the New Year of 1951, Frank Laubach and I decided to hold our own Congress because the other Congress was bewildered! There, in a great downtown church, we began to organize our own Department of Peace and in the words of Frank Laubach, "declare a War of Astonishing Kindness and plan an assault of unselfish deeds upon the world."

One of our first undertakings was to create a Spiritual Embassy in our Capital City. To house our Department of Peace we purchased a building in Washington where people of all faiths and all denominations can come and pray for the government or arrange to meet with their senators and representatives at stated times. In this capacious building the leaders of the Washington prayer groups and others interested in prayer will meet at least once a month in a School of Prayer. Every time Congress convenes there will be someone in the gallery of both Senate and House praying for their deliberations to be guided by God. Each Congressman and Senator will also have a number of people especially appointed to concentrate in prayer for him. In innumerable ways this Spiritual Embassy Building will be made the center for focusing the prayers of all the praying groups of the nation upon the President and the leaders of Congress and the various departments of government. From it will be issued each month a *News Sheet for Those Who Pray*.

The Department of War carries on its functions by means of an Infantry Force, an Artillery Force and an Air Force. In place of the Air Force our Department of Peace will be supported by a Prayer Force; in place of an Artillery Force we shall have a Corps of Message Bringers; while the Infantry Force will be made up of earnest sincere Christian "foot soldiers" who are doing God's work in their homes, factories or wherever they happen to be.

There are thousands of prayer groups all over the nation to furnish the Prayer Force, and one of the under-secretaries of the Department of Peace will supervise the formation of many more, keeping in touch with them all as far as possible so they may be enlisted for special service at any time of crisis. One important branch of this Prayer Force consists of the army of shut-ins, veterans in hospitals and people in old folks' homes who have plenty of leisure. These will form one of the most vital battalions that can be found to pray with power for the peace of the world. We feel that just these untapped reserves when properly marshalled and brought into action might turn the tide of destiny toward peace.

Another under-secretary will keep track of the move-

ment of the Message Bringers so that they will not all
bombard the same town at the same time. By bringing
these flying squadrons into action at the right time and
the right place, city after city will be taken over by the
forces of peace. At this point our Department is singularly well-equipped. We have a well-trained battalion of
spiritual veterans with especial gifts for awakening folks
to the deepening of the spiritual life, available to invade
any territory wherever the need calls. Preceded by a bar-
rage of prayer from hidden prayer nests all over the nation, these veteran campaigners can march into any city,
coming in waves one after another until all its strategic
centers are taken. Then in departing they can leave as
a garrison a thriving Christ for Others Group capable
of holding all the ground that was gained, and mopping
up the areas where more work is needed. These city
strongholds of Prayer furnish the landing fields for the
Messengers of Light to get footholds in the cities and
recruiting grounds of old and young for the camps and
training schools.

As one important function of the War Department is
to work out plans for co-operating with allies abroad for
the winning of wars, our Department of Peace is co-
operating with spiritual leaders in foreign lands for the
winning of peace. Friends are planning several Religious Odyssey Tours for us to foreign lands where spiritual retreats with Christian groups will be interspersed
between periods of sight-seeing, thus building bridges for
international understanding and co-operation and friendship on the highest levels.

As the War Department has base camps for training
their recruits, our Department of Peace is already conducting between twenty and thirty training camps care-

fully distributed in every section of the country throughout the months of spring, summer and fall where people can be trained in the disciplines and release to be found in the spiritual life, where they can experience its joy and contagion, and where they can learn to pray with power.

The War Department has a West Point as a year round institution for the training of officers, and the Peace Department has also acquired a "Spiritual West Point" for the training of spiritual leaders. West Point on the Hudson has no more attractive setting than our Koinonia Training Center, located in one of the most beautiful areas just outside of Baltimore. Those capable of reading the handwriting on the wall are aware that unless our nations turn to God we stand in imminent peril. I would urge young men and women who are considering a political, scientific or professional career to attend one of these training camps, or better still, to spend a year at Koinonia, the Spiritual West Point for training ambassadors of the Spirit.

Lest people get the notion that this concentration on the power of prayer and the power of love is some scatterbrained escapist philosophy of impractical dreamers we are undergirding this entire Department of Peace with the soundest foundations of scientific research. One of the most famous universities of America undertook a few years ago to prove beyond the question of doubt the reality of telepathy and the scientific laws underlying it. The scientists engaged in that research at this great university are now working hand in hand with our Department of Peace in exploring and determining the significance and reality of prayer and the great fundamental laws by which it works. Our training camps that deal with prayer are serving as their field laboratories for experimentation and field research. Having discovered, for instance, the law by which the Hopi Indians are able to bring rain through prayer, we are now exploring how the methods of Jesus when properly employed by a sufficient number of dedicated people might bring peace to the world through prayer.

As the War Department has its staff for publicity and propaganda, our Department of Peace is well-equipped for the distribution of literature of the spirit. A nationally known publishing house, publishing a quarterly magazine dedicated to this work, has a large force busy filling thousands of orders coming in each week from all over the country for books on prayer and the deepening of the spiritual life. Over half its profits go to the underwriting of this movement.

You are urged to enlist in this army which is going to work joyfully and rhythmically to develop a Department of Peace to balance (in dynamic symmetry) our government's Department of War.* When this Department of Peace has established itself a little longer and proved to the leaders of the nation what such activities could do for peace and national well being, the government may wish to assume some of the responsibility of carrying on a similar program but on a much larger scale. When national and individual efforts work hand in hand we can then feel assured that permanent peace shall actually come to this world.

* If interested write Department of Peace Religious Embassy Building, 1707 19th St. N. W. Washington, D. C.

FOREWORD TO PART IV

When one views life from the higher dimensions he discovers that there is only one Being in all the universe and that one is *God;* there is only one Emotion and that is *Love;* there is only one *Time* and that is the Eternal *Now;* there is only one Space and that is the Infinite *Here;* and finally, there is only one Motion and that is the motion to keep in balance with all these other Ones.

Perfection of any kind or of every kind is attained when one enters into the center of all those "Ones" at the same time. For instance, when you are entertaining no emotion but the emotion of Love—so perfectly filled with it that there is no room for fear or resentments or anything else—then you know what bliss is. If you are content in the Now with no regrets over the past and no worries for the future you know what joy is. If you are content in the Here with no envy or yearning for places where you are not supposed to be you know what peace is. In other words when you are content with the motionless motion of resting in the Love of God in the Here and Now you are experiencing heaven.

"Seek first the Kingdom of Heaven and all these things will be added unto you." Seek first, said Jesus, in effect, this Kingdom of perfect equilibrium, this Kingdom of perfect rest, and all things will come to you in perfect sequence and perfect order.

This Kingdom of heaven is ours the moment we step into these four *Ones* all at the same time. As it is difficult for a novice in golf to remember all four rules he must obey at each stroke, and as it is equally difficult to drive four horses abreast, so one cannot expect to step into this Kingdom of Oneness without long practice. But once attained it is the simplest and the most natural way to live that there is. When we let our emotions split up from one into many, when we begin to worry about the future that never comes, when we become impatient to move to other places we have never seen, when we begin to make all kinds of restless, unmeaning motions that throw us out of balance with God, then it is that we become exposed to all the confusions this world falls heir to.

Perfect equilibrium, on the other hand, is yours when all your little motions are subordinated to the One Great Motion of keeping in balance with God in the Here and Now, and all your little emotions are subordinated to the Great Emotion of unselfish Love. Then you won't need to seek ideas, Love will draw them to you in perfect sequence and perfect order; you won't have to seek people for Love will draw just the right ones to you when you want to see them; you won't have to seek for riches, for Love will draw your daily bread to you as you need it without the bother of storing it up for weeks in advance. If you look carefully at that masterpiece, the Lord's Prayer, you will find that Jesus there lays down this pattern of perfect equilibrium with God in words you can never forget.

This kind of equilibrium is never monotonous, for there is no monotony in Love. You will find no boredom in this complete oneness, for as the white light of the sun, when passing through a prismatic lens, is broken up into the seven tints of the rainbow, so Love, to reach every area and meet every need of mankind, is broken up into the octave of reverence, adoration, compassion, forgiveness, comradeship, affection, loyalty and co-operation. When one starts playing on this octave he experiences the Music of the Spheres.

Abiding in that perfect Love of the One God, in his perfect Here and his perfect Now you will realize an inward Bliss you never experienced before, for you will be abiding in that *Rest* described in the 4th chapter of Hebrews, in that *Trust* described in the 91st Psalm, and that *Peace* described in the 6th chapter of Matthew. You will find yourself in equilibrium with all that ever was, ever is or ever shall be, where all mistakes of the past will be forgotten; where you will be impervious to any dangers of the present or future, and where there will be no enemies, but only friends.

PART IV

Adventuring in the Higher Dimensions

CHAPTER XVIII

Beneath Activity Lies Stillness

AFTER writing *The Soul's Sincere Desire,* I tried the experiment of living for an entire year in the fifth, sixth and seventh dimensions; in other words, I definitely tried to put myself in such alignment with God and in such rhythm with mankind that I could live in the four Ones, all at the same time.

How did I do it? As the drop of water in the mud puddle is drawn out of its sordid environment by the simple act of giving itself unresistingly to the drawing power of the sun's rays, in a similar way I was drawn out of the confusion of this three dimensional world by the simple act of giving myself unresistingly to the drawing power of the infinite, unlimited love of God.

In the next chapter I shall try to give some of the details by which this elevation was brought about; let it suffice at this point to say that to rise to this higher dimension, the one element that seemed most necessary was to surrender completely, totally, utterly, to the highest I knew and get very still. The strange paradoxical thing about this surrender and this stillness was that out of the surrender came power; out of the stillness came activity. The stiller I got, the more active I became, an activity that was amazingly free from all self-conscious effort.

Never did I move so rapidly as I did then, never did I speak so fluently, write so easily, meet people so effectively, do so much, accomplish so much. And yet I seemingly did nothing. I merely stood still in the midst of a great stillness.

And how could I accomplish so much by doing nothing? Perhaps it was because through my surrender I had so completely entered into Christ's stillness, so immersed myself in it, so identified myself with it, that I partook of the qualities of the One to whom I had surrendered. And as it was a great, unlimited, infinite stillness, perhaps I, too, became unlimited and infinite. At any rate, it was not until I had become one with that stillness that I became aware of what true infinity is.

When one steps into that seventh dimensional stillness he seems to be everywhere at once. Wherever the need draws him, behold he is there; wherever there is that which he needs, behold he is there. Space is blotted out, Time is blotted out. The past is in him, the present is in him, the future is in him. Whatever idea has been known in the past is available for him. But he does nothing except stand still in the midst of a vast stillness, and power and knowledge become his.

Many years ago you were a little child. As time rolls on you become an adult, aged and ripe in years. But you were always a child, and you are one now. You were always an adult ripe in years, and are one now. Viewed from the higher dimensions there need be no past or future; there is only one time and that is the Eternal NOW. Viewed from the lower dimensions the world seems to stretch to the east and to the west, to the north and to the south, but viewed from above there appears only one space—the Infinite HERE.

Wordsworth in "Tintern Abbey" was able to shut out the clamor of this three dimensional world by withdrawing from the haunts of man and contemplating the harmonious beauties of Nature:

"These beauteous forms,
    Through a long absence, have not been to me
    As is a landscape to a blind man's eye:
    But oft in lonely rooms, and 'mid the din
    Of towns and cities, I have owed to them
    In hours of weariness, sensations sweet
    Felt in the blood, and felt along the heart;
    And passing even into my purer mind,
    With tranquil restoration:—feelings too
    Of unremembered pleasure; such, perhaps,
    As have no slight or trivial influence
    On that best portion of a good man's life,
    His little, nameless, unremembered acts
    Of kindness and of love. Nor less, I trust,
    To them I may have owed another gift,
    Of aspect more sublime; that blessed mood,
    In which the heavy and the weary weight
    Of all this unintelligible world,
    Is lightened;—that serene and blessed mood,
    In which the affections gently lead us on,—
    Until the breath of this corporeal frame
    And even the motion of our human blood
    Almost suspended, we are laid asleep
    In body, and become a living soul:
    While with an eye made quiet by the power
    Of harmony, and the deep power of joy
    We see into the life of things.

    For I have learned
    To look on nature, not as in the hour
    Of thoughtless youth; but hearing oftentimes
    The still, sad music of humanity,
    Nor harsh nor grating, though of ample power

> To chasten and subdue. And I have felt
> A presence that disturbs me with the joy
> Of elevated thoughts; a sense sublime
> Of something far more deeply interfused,
> Whose dwelling is the light of setting suns,
> And the round ocean and the living air,
> And the blue sky, and in the mind of man;
> A motion and a spirit, that impels
> All thinking things, all objects of all thought,
> And rolls through all things."

Tennyson was able to shut out the confusion of this three dimensional world by focusing all his mind, heart and senses upon a little flower:

> "Flower in the crannied wall,
> I pluck you out of the crannies,
> I hold you here, root and all, in my hand,
> Little flower—but *if* I could understand
> What you are, root and all, and all in all,
> I should know what God and man is."

One day I asked the question: As I am not a Wordsworth or a Tennyson, how can I reconcile the seeming fragmentariness of life and these fleeting glimpses of it offered me, with this inner awareness of the Infinite Here and the Eternal Now? Clear as a bell came the answer:

"God in his great love and kindness knows that the Infinite Here and the Everlasting Now are too big for you to see all at once and therefore he is unfolding them to you in a perfect sequence and a perfect order that has been arranged for you in heaven. All you need do is trust to that order and sequence, trust all things to unfold according to God's perfect plan—and STAND STILL."

And when I trusted this voice and stood still I seemed to move more rapidly through the world than the world had ever seen me move before. I found it impossible to account for this increased efficiency in my life that seemed to come from merely standing still until I turned in meditation one day to the mystery of a train running on its track.

Let us imagine that we are on a train that is carrying us to distant parts. Everything is arranged according to law and order. When time comes to eat, a waiter gives the call for dinner. When time comes to sleep, a porter makes our seat into a bed. The schedule is so planned that we are carried through the beautiful scenery in the daytime and through the less interesting portions at night.

But suppose we do not trust the plan of the journey. Suppose we believe we are being cheated by the Master Planner who has plotted out the trip. We shall therefore lie awake all night to see the scenery which is being hidden from us behind the curtain of darkness. We shall then be so drowsy in the daytime that we shall nap when passing the great canyon or beautiful mountain. We may not trust the sufficiency of the table d'hôte dinner promised for the evening, and may nibble on popcorn and candy all afternoon and then be unable to eat at night the wonderful banquet laid before us. We may disarrange the beautiful order and sequence which the great Master has planned, but the order and sequence will remain. Others will find it. Because we happen to sleep during the day does not mean that the beautiful mountain is not there. Because we are unable to eat our dinner doesn't mean that abundance to satisfy our needs is not there.

We might even rebel against going to the destination which has been planned for us—the beautiful and glorious destination which outshines our fondest dreams. We may pull down our curtains and not look out of the window and try to make believe the train is not moving.

We may turn our back on our destination and walk away from it. Little do we know that even while walking away from our destination we are actually moving toward it. If we walk far enough, we shall come to the end of the train, and shall have to return again to the comfortable seat that has been arranged for us.

Thus our little rebellions will serve us naught, except to confuse the journey, waste our time, make us miss meeting people who are seeking us, miss scenery that would charm us, miss abundance of food and comfort and rest that has been prepared for us! Why try to flee from it, why try to disarrange it or supplant it with little, spiteful plans of our own? Why not simply sit still and abide in peace and calmness and move easily, smoothly, rhythmically onward in harmony with the Great Plan?

This is not mere fancy. We are all traveling through life on a train, but the train we ride on is a train of the inner consciousness. Some day we may learn that there is no movement in the world at all, excepting in the consciousness. And the consciousness moves from point to point in the great vastness which God has given us, from period and peak and pinnacle to period and peak and pinnacle. *But we ourselves do not move.*

When we go in perfect harmony with the Great Planner's Plan we see all the beautiful scenery of the universe and enjoy all the comforts of the journey. When we are not in harmony with Him we fail to see or to enjoy that which was meant for us to see and enjoy. And yet the journey is the same journey, whether we enjoy it or rebel against it. For all our rebellion and distrust cannot destroy one whit of its marvelous beauty, happiness and comfort. We may, through our distrust, miss seeing the scenery. That is all. But even if we miss it, it is there.

After abiding in this stillness where everything I did was completely free of all self-conscious effort, I made a great discovery: Time and Space are two toys which God has given to man with which he amuses himself while waiting outside the Garden of Heaven. Whenever man puts on the colored glasses of Space, his entire life on earth appears as a constantly *moving* process; whenever he puts on the colored glasses of Time, his life on earth appears as a constantly *growing* process. Through the lens of Space everything appears to be coming and going; through the lens of Time everything seems to be growing and decaying.

But are the angels in heaven pestered by all this coming and going? Are they bothered by all this growing and de-caying?

Suppose that for a moment we took off the spectacles of Time and Space and saw the world as the angels in heaven see it, as a simple Temple in the midst of Infinity and Eternity. It would then be revealed to us, in the twinkling of an eye, that all the Love that ever was, that ever is, that ever will be, exists at this very moment, is everywhere present and is instantly available whenever we need it or seek it; that all the friends we need or crave are seeking us; that all the sunshine we need is already out there coming continually from the solar rays; that all the gas and oil and coal is under our feet, waiting to be mined when the need calls; that all the poems, sym-phonies and sonatas are waiting for us deep in the mind of man, instantly available when the poet or composer calls.

True, these riches within ourselves or within the earth or within the ethers do not come at every haphazard call. They seem to await some inner, inscrutable Plan worked out in the blueprints of the Master Planner. But whenever we put ourselves in tune with the Divine Plan of this Master Planner all things seem able to come to us in perfect sequence and perfect order, in exactly the right way, at exactly the right time. We must be peaceful and patient: peaceful because our present need will be filled; patient because tomorrow's need will not be filled till tomorrow. Yes, Catherine Mendenhall is right:

> "Time is a Teacher; and Space is a Friend;
> To keep us from traveling too fast and too far.
> We have to learn Patience and then we can blend
> With the Time and the Place wherever we are."

CHAPTER XIX

Beneath Confusion Lies the Perfect Pattern

IN THE beginning of the last chapter it was promised that in this chapter would be given some of the details regarding methods that proved helpful in lifting me into the higher dimensions.

I began with the very simple experiment of denying the despotic totalitarianism of this three dimensional realm, and affirming the spaceless and timeless realities of the higher dimensional realm. I discovered that the reason why the 23rd Psalm was the most loved prayer in the world, adopted by Hindus, Buddhists and Mohammedans as well as by Jews, Catholics and Protestants, was because it is the perfect instrument for doing exactly that thing.

The Lord is my Shepherd:	*I shall not want.*
I shall not want for peace:	*He maketh me to lie down in green pastures.*
I shall not want for security:	*He leadeth me beside the still waters,*
I shall not want for healing:	*He restoreth my soul.*
I shall not want for guidance:	*He leadeth me in paths of righteousness, for His name's sake.*
The Lord is my Shepherd:	*I shall fear no evil.*
I shall fear no evil from death:	*For Thou art with me in the valley and the shadow.*

I shall fear no evil from danger:	*For Thy rod and Thy staff shall protect me.*
I shall fear no evil from famine:	*For Thou preparest a table before me.*
I shall fear no evil from enemies:	*For Thou preparest a table before me in the presence of mine enemies.*
I shall fear no evil from mental disturbances:	*Thou anointest my head with oil.*
I shall fear no evil from want:	*My cup runneth over.*
I shall fear no evil from sin:	*Surely goodness and mercy shall follow me all the days of my life.*
I shall fear no evil from separation from my Heavenly Father.	*I shall dwell in the house of the Lord forever.*

Expanding on this principle, I wrote the psalm-prayers now found in the last chapter of *The Soul's Sincere Desire*. My way of shutting off the outer three dimensional world and concentrating upon the perfect realities in the upper dimensions was: I would hold the sheet containing a psalm-prayer in my hands, thus concentrating on it the sense of touch; I would read it with my eyes, thus utilizing the sense of sight; I would read it aloud, thus exercising the sense of taste; I would hear it with my ears, thus using the sense of hearing. If I had dropped some incense upon it I would have used all five senses so completely in this rite of the spirit that the whole outer world would have been blotted out.

For instance I would read this psalm aloud.

A PSALM OF LOVE

Thou and Thy Love are infinite;
Thy Love therefore fills all space,
There is no space where Thy Love is not,
Otherwise it would not be infinite.
It is filling the very space which we are occupying,
Here and Now.

That Love is in us and we are in that Love.
We could not escape it if we would,
And we would not if we could.
It abides in us and we in it.
Therefore when we let go doubt, and irritation, and self,
And resign ourselves completely to the great All-Power
That resides within and about us,
We *are* Love, even as God is Love.

God then speaks through us,
Thinks through us, acts through us;
For when we speak, we speak Love,
When we think, we think Love,
When we create, we create Love;
For God always does His work by means of Love made manifest in man.

After reading this aloud once or twice until I was positively filled and charged with Love, I could walk past dangerous bulldogs—yes, I believe I could have entered a lion's cage and no creature would have hurt me.

Other days I would read the other psalm-prayers on inspiration, wholeness or gratitude, whatever the need for me might be. I found these psalm-prayers especially effective in "Charging" me so full of love, faith, joy, and gratitude, that wonderful things began to occur every day in my life. The drawing power that lifted me so powerfully in these psalm-prayers finds its perfect expression in these living words of Christ:

"Abide in Me, and I in you. As the branch cannot bear fruit of itself except it abide in the vine; no more can ye, except ye abide in Me. Henceforth, I call you not servants, for the servant knoweth not what his lord doeth; but I have called you friends; for all things that I have heard of My Father I have made known unto you. Ye have not chosen Me, but I have chosen you, and ordained you, that ye should go and bring forth fruit, and that your fruit should remain: That whatsoever ye shall ask of the Father in My name, He may give it you!" (John 15:4, 15, 16)

And I found great peace in this prayer of my own creating:

"Our Heavenly Father, henceforth we shall have no fear, for we trust utterly in Thee, and Thou art the God of Love, Giver of every good and perfect gift. Resting in Thee, and abiding eternally in Thy love, we are impervious as in a citadel, for no evil can henceforth reach us without first passing through Thee, being transformed in the process into perfect purity, perfect harmony, and perfect love. Hold us close to Thy heart, O Father, and accept our gratitude, our adoration, and our love. Amen."

Finally I focused all these discoveries into the one—to me—tremendous discovery of God's Divine Plan for each of us, the contemplation and acceptance of which did more to lift me into the higher dimensions than anything that had come to me outside of Jesus Himself.

I would advise my reader to accept this Divine Plan as a positive reality; believe it as an affirmation of truth; read it aloud if possible, so you can taste it and hear it at the same time you are feeling it with your hands and seeing it with your eyes. For a few minutes each day let it enlist all your senses, all your mind, all your emotions, all your will and see what happens at the end of three weeks. See if your ladder is turning into a stairway and your stairway into an elevator, and your elevator into a helicopter lifting you into a new world—or an old world turned new!

I. I believe that God has a Divine Plan for me. I believe that this Plan is wrapped in the folds of my Being, even as the oak is wrapped in the acorn and the rose is wrapped in the bud. I believe that this Plan is permanent, indestructible, and perfect, free from all that is essentially bad. Whatever comes into my life that is negative is not a part of this God-created Plan, but is a distortion caused by my failure to harmonize myself with the Plan as God has made it. I believe that this Plan is Divine, and when I relax myself completely to it, it will manifest completely and perfectly through me. I can always tell when I am completely relaxed to the Divine Plan by the inner peace that comes to me. This inner peace brings a joyous, creative urge that leads me into activities that unfold the Plan, or it brings a patience and a stillness that allow others to unfold the Plan to me.

II. I believe that this beautiful Divine Plan for me is a perfect part of the larger Pattern for the good of all, not something separate unto me alone. I believe that it has ramifications and interweavings that reach out through all the persons that I meet and all the events that come to me, and that the best way to put myself in harmony with the Divine Plan that is within myself is to accept with radiant acquiescence all the individuals and events that are drawn to me, seeing in them perfect instruments for the perfect unfoldment of my perfect Plan. In other words, I believe that to see harmony in that which is without brings harmony in that which is within, even as to see harmony in that which is within brings harmony in that which is without.

III. I believe that God has selected those persons who are to belong to my plan, and that through proximity, mutual attraction or need, they and I are continually finding each other out. I believe in praying for ever-increasing capacity to love and serve them and for greater worthiness to be loved and served by them in return. I believe in sending out a prayer to the Father to draw to me those who are meant to help me and to be helped by me, in order to express my life together with them.

IV. I believe in asking my Heavenly Father for only that which is mine to have, knowing that when the right time has come it will be made manifest. This enables me to look forward to receiving only those things which are mine according to the Providential Plan. It releases my mind from all anxiety and uncertainty. It eliminates fear, jealousy, and anger. It gives me courage and faith to do the things that are mine to do. When my mind is attuned to the things that are mine, I become free from greed, passion, impure thoughts and deeds; but when I look without or watch others to see what they are or are not receiving, I cut myself off from my own source of supply and minimize my power to receive.

V. I believe that the gifts of God are many thousands of times greater than I am now capable of receiving, and that I should therefore pray to increase my capacity both to receive and to give, for my power to receive is as great as my power to give, and my power to give as to receive. Gifts of God always bring peace, contentment and joy, and therefore anything in which I find a natural harmony and peace and which does not interfere with anyone else's natural expression of life belongs to me, and any work for which I feel a natural call, by gift or inclination, is mine to do. When I am attuned to that which is mine I find no barrier in God's Kingdom, hence I accept none.

VI. I believe that God's Plan for life is a healthy happy expression for the good of all, and that everything that makes me feel happy to do will bring happiness to others. Therefore, when I am hindered from doing the thing that I want to do, I believe that God has closed the door only to open another, and that upon every closed door there is a sign pointing to a better and larger door just ahead. My disappointments, therefore, become His appointments. If I do not readily see the door just ahead, I believe that is because there is some blindness, deafness or disobedience within my life that walls me off from God and that God is using the resulting trouble or failure to help me find the inspiration and the guidance and the power to help overcome it so that I may see the right door.

VII. I believe that the chief essential of life is to keep in touch with the Father, and let the Divinity that is in me manifest through me. I believe that the whole world about me is full of beauty, joy, and power, even as it is full of God, and that I can share it and enjoy it if I attune myself to my Divine Plan and am inwardly open toward God and outwardly helpful toward men. I shall ask my Heavenly Father and Friend, who dwells within me and who has given me this vision of life, to give me His help in its realization and to help me share it with others that it may bring peace and happiness to many.*

* This Divine Plan, slightly modified, under the title "God's Plan" is today being translated into all languages and being sent to all peoples of all religions the world over. Anyone wishing samples of these, or desirous of helping finance this amazing movement may write Box 248 Madison Square Station, New York, N. Y.

CHAPTER XX

Beyond Time Lies Eternity

ONE DARK night I was leaving a car in a neighbor's garage. A few feet from the door of the garage was staked a vicious bulldog which was leaping passionately at me to the full extent of his chain. I was on the point of padlocking the door and starting for home, when I suddenly KNEW the dog would break his chain within the next five seconds. I removed the padlock and stepped inside the garage and pulled the door to after me. At that instant the chain broke and the dog plunged futilely against the closed door.

In the winter of 1923 two students asked me why I was so sure that we would not have a war with Japan that year. I asked God to furnish the answer and I suddenly heard my lips saying to them, "Because Japan will be destroyed by an earthquake within the next six months." Five months after this the great Japanese earthquake occurred.

Here were forewarnings, in the first place of five seconds, in the second place of five months. What did the difference of time matter? The larger events, like the larger mountains, seem to loom higher in perspective and therefore are more readily discernible in the far distance than the smaller events. That is all. But in every case the thin partition between present and future was wiped out, and all time became one.

Of course, I am not alone in this experience. Not long before his death, Luther Burbank told in a magazine article how for one hundred mornings he awoke with perfect knowledge of every event that was going to happen to him during the day, in exactly the way and order in which it was going to happen. Burbank believed with his whole being that Time was as fluid as Space, and he therefore accomplished in a few years what otherwise would have required a millennium. He stepped up the creation of fruits and flowers which, if mankind had awaited the slow evolutionary processes of Nature, we should not have known for centuries.

But Space was not always fluid in the consciousness of man. There was a time, and that was not long ago, when it was the solidest kind of solid substance, even more solid than our present day conception of Time. To cross a continent required the long-drawn-out agony and untold hardship of ox team and covered wagon. Rivers were unfordable, mountains were impassable, and letters were few and far between. Newspapers were carried by pony express riders. Telegraph, telephone and television were unknown. A man a thousand miles away from his brothers was in another world—a banished man. The solid barriers of the solid substance, Space separated mankind into isolated units, each group shut off to itself. In that era of solid Space the world was simply crammed full of skeptics and agnostics regarding the possibility of ever rendering it a fluid. They would have dismissed as a madman's dream the hint that a flying machine could ever carry a man through the air at the rate of over 700 miles an hour. They would have thought it preposterous even to hint at the possibility of hearing another man's voice a thousand miles away.

Within fifty years all these miracles in conquering Space have come to pass. But the skeptics and agnostics are still with us. They have merely transferred their skepticism and agnosticism from the fluidity of Space to the fluidity of Time. Fifty years ago they scoffed at the possibility of an event, such as a boxing match or an inauguration, being announced in all its detail to an audience a thousand miles away. Today they scoff at the possibility of such an event being announced in detail to an audience removed from them by a thousand weeks. And yet, what is the difference? Are not Time and Space merely twin devices given us by which we may chart and bring under control the immensities of Infinity and Eternity which stretch forth without us and within us?

Space stretches off to the right and to the left, up and down, into Infinity. Time stretches off before and behind us into Eternity. There is no limit to Space and there is no limit to Time. They are all there, but we normally see only as much of either of them as is passing within the radius of our experience right HERE and NOW.

Our senses, inasmuch as they are normal and perfect, are the end-organs by which we detect the presence of objects in Space. Our dreams and our desires, insofar as they are the expression of *real* aspirations and *real* needs of our inner soul, are the end organs by which we detect the presence of events ahead of us in Time. When our ears are arrested by a sound of falling water, and our eyes are disturbed by the appearance of mists ahead, we know we are approaching the rapids. When our hearts are filled with a vague foreboding or our imaginations are caught up with the glimpse of a Utopian dream, we can know that an old enemy or a new friend is coming toward us down the corridors of Time.

But our dreams and desires are surely not as true and infallible as our sense of sight and sense of sound, says someone! Whoever said that our senses were infallible? In this age so rampant with astigmatism, far-sightedness, near-sightedness and color blindness; in this age of deafness, is it not reasonable to expect some astigmatism and color blindness in our dreams and desires? But even then it is not the senses that are wrong nearly as often as our minds, nor is it our desires and dreams that carry us awry nearly as often as it is our souls. The keenest senses will not guide a man aright who has a disordered mind; neither will the most eager desires and the most vivid dreams guide a man aright who has a disordered soul.

One of the chief requirements we demand of the railroad engineer who is to conduct us on a journey is that he be a total abstainer from anything which would cloud his mind. We do not want to commit our lives to the control of a man whose mind is drunk, and who, when his eyesight sees red, misinterprets it as green and drives us into a wreck. A clear mind is far more necessary than clear senses. In the same way, ninety-nine times out of one hundred if we have a clear soul we can let our dreams and desires take care of themselves.

Put your mind and emotions in order and your senses will guide you aright. Put your souls in order and your dreams and desires will guide you aright. But if your souls are askew, when you dream of abundance, you will demand satiety; when you dream of service you will demand fame; when you desire the opportunity to share, you will demand possession; when you dream of peace and stillness, you will demand sloth and lethargy; when you dream of bliss you will demand pleasure. And to put your soul in order is to bring it into alignment with the Plan of the Great Master Planner, and into rhythm with the true needs of all mankind, and let it rest in stillness in the midst of the great stillness of God.

The time has come when we should make the same demands of those selected to lead us on political, religious and educational journeys that we have made in the past of those who lead us on our journeys through Space—for is not our mental, social and national welfare as essential as our physical? And as we refuse to let our trains be piloted by men with maudlin minds, neither should we let our nations be governed by men with maudlin souls. The time has come when we should demand of the nation as we demand of the individual, *put your soul in order.*

If the purpose of this book were to carry my readers up to the fourth dimension and stop there I would not have included this chapter in the book. Precognition of the future is a psychic gift that comes only to people who have risen as high as the fourth dimension, but if they stop there they will confuse the conception of God's perfect plan with fatalism. Fatalism means that man is going down a blind alley and that what is ahead of him is ahead of him and no amount of thinking, praying, or anything else will prevent his *running straight into it.* That is certainly not God's way of doing things. In His perfect Plan you have all eternity to move about in, and there is no excuse for running into blind alleys.

As we lengthen and amplify our sense of sight and hearing, through the radio and wireless, we are able to hear of storms and washouts ahead of us in our journeys, and are thus able to avoid disaster on our journeys through Space. Is it not equally reasonable to assume by lengthening and amplifying the quality of our dreams and desires through prayer we may become aware of approaching evil in time to avoid it in our journey through Time?

The moment you step up into the fifth, sixth, and seventh dimensions you will see that this is not fatalism—it is not even predestination, excepting insofar as you are predestined for good. Fatalism is where a man with blindfolded eyes goes down a dangerous road with outstretched hands and straining ear, completely at the mercy of any object coming toward him. The higher divination I am writing about comes when men move forward with all bandages removed and the area of foresight so greatly increased that they can avoid all necessity of accident. When that day of fore-knowledge arrives we shall find that it will be for mankind the actual beginning of free will. True freedom never comes to man until he faces the future with perfect trust in God, perfect love for men, and perfect faith in prayer.

If in Space you could rise to a great height and see a burning city ahead, would you have to run right into it? Supposing you are riding across the country and see a stone wall, or a steep cliff ahead, will you dash against the wall or fall over the cliff? Or would you, because of your fore-knowledge, change your course?

Who said we ever had to go on into anything, or bump against anything? All the bad things we foresee are there for us to avoid. They are there for us to try to remedy, to overcome, or, failing in that, to flee from. And how? By turning. Turning where? To God. That is exactly what three-fourths of the troubles ahead of us are for—not something for us to run into, but something for us to avoid *by turning to God. They are, in short, nothing more or less than signposts pointing us to God.*

The flood was foretold to Noah. He could not stop the flood but he could build an ark. The burning of Sodom was foretold to Lot. He could not stop the burning but he could flee away in time. And each could take with him such of his family and friends who would hear the voice of God speaking through him and obey it. All the men, women and children in the time of Noah could have escaped the flood if they had turned to God. All the men, women and children in the day of Lot could have escaped the fire if they had turned to God. And our entire nation when confronted with World War III can escape if we turn to God. The purpose of prophecy in the Old Testament was not to tell the kings what was inevitable, but what was inevitable if they went forward without turning to God at every crossroads.

To foresee, then, is not so important as acting wisely after we foresee. One is the means, the other the end. If you get the end without the means you do not need the means. If you get the means without the end your labor is dust and ashes. To *prophesy* is not the big thing the world needs—to *turn* is what the world needs. The little prophets gave themselves to the excitement of prophecy, some of them actually became lost in the thrill of being able to foresee the future and forgot to go on to the greater and the more essential end for which the prophecy was intended—to turn to God in the Present. But the great prophets prophesied little and gave much attention to interpreting the meaning of the warning for which the prophecy stood: "To love mercy, do justly and walk humbly with thy God."

I should like to close this chapter with reference again to the prophecy of a World War III. It happens to synchronize with the purpose for which this has been written, and thus becomes a clarion call to the nation to *turn to God*. It becomes an announcement that it is time for statesmen and rulers, not of this nation only, but of the world as a whole, to give up their false gods of Materialism and turn to the only *true God,* the *God* of the *Kingdom that is within,* for counsel and guidance. The time has come when the rulers of our nation instead of taking as their only advisers and counsellors the so-called practical business men and politicians, should take as counsellors and advisers the prophets and seers, for assistance in guiding the counsels of the nation.

It is time for the rulers not to seek to pry into the future, for the future will take care of itself, but to seek to find the Kingdom of God and its righteousness, knowing that when they have once found this and taken this into their statecraft and into their kingcraft, all other things will be added unto them.

CHAPTER XXI

Beyond This Life Lies Life Everlasting

WHEN one has lived a while in the seventh dimension he absolutely knows that death is not the end of our individual existence, but is merely the completion of the first stage in life, marking the close of one's seed time, and the beginning of his harvest time. Man's budding hopes, his lofty aspirations, his dreams and desires which no earthly fulfillment can satisfy, are but the seed-germs that are to blossom and bear immortal fruit in the Eternity that lies ahead. Man leaves in the grave only the swaddling clothes of his spiritual infancy and arises as from sleep in his perfect stature in which hope is turned into fruition, and aspiration to attainment. My faith in immortality is built upon such solid foundations that I want to share these foundations with you now.

I. The first proof of immortality is the simple, psychological fact that where God has planted a yearning in the human heart, he has somewhere planted a supply to meet that yearning. Men thirst for water, and water is found flowing down from the mountains and bursting through the springs. Men's lungs crave oxygen, and air surrounds them to supply it in unlimited amounts.

Man has an inordinate craving for immortality, even as the squirrel has a craving for nuts. I believe that as truly as God furnishes the acorns to fulfill the craving of a squirrel, he will furnish the immortality to fulfill the craving in the hearts of human beings. Are not we worth more than many squirrels?

II. The second proof I offer is one drawn from nature. The evening that followed the simple funeral services in our little church in honor of my wife, a car drove up in front of my house. Dr. George Washington Carver came to see me. He said, "Your dear wife, while seemingly absent now, is actually closer to you than ever before. You will feel her presence more than ever. But where she has been a staff to you in the past, now she will be wings. The butterfly is the most spiritual of nature's beings. It could not exist however unless the little worm that it had formerly been had been willing to go through a transformation process by which it—the worm—ceased to exist. Your wife has merely passed through this transformation process. Now she, too, has wings." Nothing is more true than that our body is but the chrysalis stage of our existence; death is but a birth into another life.

I sat at my wife's bedside when my first child was born. A few years later I sat at my father's bedside as his spirit took its departure for the other world. I had a strange mystic experience in both cases and it was revealed to me in those hours that birth throes and death throes are one and the same thing. Only, strange to say, I felt a greater relief, a greater ecstasy, greater sense of liberation as I experienced the soul of my father rising to heaven than I did when my child was being brought to earth. Yes, the birth into the world and the birth out of it are twin processes, but with this difference, so beautifully expressed by the Persian proverb, "When a man is born he begins to die, when he dies he begins to live."

III. Another wonderful proof of immortality I derive from the matrix of the printer, and the master die of the government mint. I have in my library a book which was the inspiration of my wife and her daughters in their childhood, and which will be a similar inspiration to their daughters and their daughters' daughters, to the third and fourth generation, indeed, as long as life shall be on this globe. It is called, *Little Women*. Our personal copy is badly worn. It is as old as I am. One more generation and it will be completely worn out.

Shall I mourn over the loss of this book when it becomes so dilapidated that we must throw it away? Will it then go out of existence, be no more? No. Even though men live only three score and ten years on this earth they manage to accumulate at least enough wisdom to take good care to see that the matrix or linotype of this book is always set up and ready so that when this old dog-eared volume is no more, they can always run off a new edition.

I hold in my pocket a little red penny worn from much use. What will happen when this cent is no longer legible enough to pass for specie? I need not worry, for there are some men down in Washington who value this cent enough to see that the matrix for running off many more is always set up and is ready to go into action. When this old copper can no longer pass as legal tender it can be shipped back to the mint in Washington; cast into the smelter and again be stamped fresh and new.

Now is it not reasonable to believe that if human beings who live and accumulate wisdom over the short period of three score years and ten so value a little book for children, yes, even a tiny little one-cent piece, so much that they take foresight to see that it shall never be lost, can we not trust the wisdom and foresight of a loving Father, whose period of existence bridges all Time and all Eternity, and know that He values us living, breathing, loving human beings far more than any man could possibly value a book or coin?

Jesus was referring to this rootage in Heaven, he was pointing out the value of this immortal and eternal part of ourselves when he said to the seventy apostles after they returned elated over their many adventures on the preaching tour, "Rejoice not that the demons are subject unto thee, rejoice rather that your NAMES are written in Heaven." As Jesus called this inner matrix or connecting point with the Infinite the *Name,* Buddha called it the *Deep Self,* the Greeks called it their *Oracle* or *Guardian Angel,* the Romans called it their *Genius,* and the Arabians called it their *Genii.* The Genii behind the lamp is the spirit of Light, which Ali Baba invoked at will.

For demonstration of this analogy in all its perfection we need only to go to those great souls who keep in close touch through inner communion with their Father Who is in Heaven.

An outstanding proof of immortality based on this rootage in Heaven I gather from Socrates. He consulted his inner matrix the morning that he was to receive the verdict of the senators. When he reached the assembly and received the verdict he was amazed to find it was Death, not Life. When asked if he had anything to say, he replied:

"My dear judges—I should like to tell you of a wonderful circumstance. Hitherto the familiar Oracle within me has constantly been in the habit of opposing me even about trifles if I was going to make a slip or error about anything; and now as you see there has come upon me that which many thought, and is generally believed to be, the last and worst evil. But the Oracle made no sign of opposition, either as I was leaving my house and going out in the morning, or when I was going up into this court, or while I was speaking, at anything which I was going to say; and yet I have often been stopped in the middle of a speech; but now in nothing I either said or did touching this matter has the Oracle opposed me. What do I take to be the explanation of this? I will tell you. I regard this as proof that what has happened to me is a good, and that those of us who think that death is an evil are in error. This is a great proof to me of what I am saying, for the customary sign would surely have opposed me had I been going to evil and not to good.

"If death is the journey to another place, and there, as men say, all the dead are, what good, O my friends and judges, can be greater than this? What would not a man give if he might converse with Orpheus and Musaeus and Hesiod and Homer? Nay, if this be true, let me die again and again. I, too, shall have a wonderful interest in a place where I can converse with Palamedes, and Ajax, the son of Telamon, and other heroes of old. What would not a man give, O judges, to be able to examine the leader of the great Trojan expedition; or Odysseus or Sisyphus, or numberless others, men and women, too? What infinite delight would there be in conversing with them and asking them questions! For in that world they do not put a man to death for this; certainly not. For being happier in that world than this, they would be immortal, if what is said is true.

"Wherefore, O judges, be of good cheer about death, and know this of a truth—that no evil can happen to a good man, either in life or after death. He and his are not neglected by the gods; nor has my own approaching end happened by mere chance. But I can see clearly that to die and be released was better for me; and therefore the Oracle gave no sign."

IV. The next proof is the question and answer method —the "Ask and it shall be given you" of Jesus. I have discovered that when two persons are completely surrendered to God and perfectly in tune with each other, when one asks the other a question of deep spiritual import, an answer of celestial significance and of absolute truth usually "comes through."

When Jesus asked Simon, "Who do you think that I am?" Simon had that experience when he said, "Thou art the Christ, the son of the living God." Jesus immediately exclaimed, "Blessed art thou, Simon Barjona; for flesh and blood hath not revealed it unto thee, but my Father which is in heaven . . . And I say unto thee, that thou are Peter, and upon this rock I will build my church, and the gates of hell shall not prevail against it." In Jesus' day, rocks served as the channels by which water was carried from the mountain tops to supply the needs of men. Substitute "channel" for "rock" and we, too, as we make ourselves clear channels, can bring the Water of Life to the souls of men.

Blithe Bonn and his associates discovered the lost abbeys of Gastonberry through the unique method of this tuning in together and with God, one asking the question while the other wrote down the answer automatically. I have had similar unique experiences which I described in *I Will Lift Up Mine Eyes.*

Job had this experience, when he asked in the fourteenth chapter of the Book of Job, "When a man die, shall he live again?" Five chapters later, after he gets quiet enough for the answer to come through, he suddenly trembles as he "feels" the answer coming through him:

"Oh that my words were now written! Oh that they were printed in a book! That they were graven with an iron pen and lead in the rock forever! For I know that my redeemer liveth and that he shall stand at the latter day upon the earth. And though after my skin worms destroy this body, yet in my flesh shall I see God: Whom I shall see for myself, and mine eyes shall behold, and not another." (Job 19:23-27)

I have known other similar experiences like this, where the realization of the reality of heaven came upon one with almost overwhelming force. One of the finest experiences of this is described by Margaret Prescott Montague in her book, *Twenty Minutes of Reality*. Anyone wanting proof of eternal life will find that little book very inspiring.*

V. My next proof of immortality came to me in a very unexpected and startling manner. A friend of mine, author of a number of books, told me one day as we looked out at the waves pounding on Star Island, off the coast of New Hampshire, of an experience she had one day as she walked past the big chair where her father usually sat when he was still on this earth. Suddenly the odor of the flowers that he especially loved filled the room. After that whenever she passed this chair the same beautiful fragrance greeted her.

"Friends coming to visit me also caught the fragrance," she continued, "and were surprised to find no flowers in the room." That led us to talking of the different loved ones that we knew who had gone on ahead. Suddenly, as we were talking, the fragrance of beautiful flowers rose

* Obtainable from Macalester Park Pub. Co.

all around us. "See," she said, "our friends shower their love on us as we talk about them."

It is strange how our five senses, geared to the outer physical world, can sometimes serve as instruments to introduce us to the unseen world. Many of my friends have heard celestial voices with their ears, or caught visions with their eyes, but it seemed amazing that the humble sense of smell could be used as an instrument of God. Especially for me, for I hardly ever notice flowers and have hardly ever given a thought to their fragrance.

It was later verified for me that those who love flowers on earth speak through them when they ascend to heaven. My son-in-law, Kermit Olsen's, grandmother had died— a great lover of flowers and gardens. At ten o'clock one night I was writing a note to her daughter, Kermit's mother, and as I did so the odor of flowers she loved simply filled the room. I assumed that my daughter had placed some flowers on my stand, and went on writing the note without bothering to look up. When I did, to my amazement, there was not a single flower in the room. The love of the dear old grandmother had broken through the walls of Eternity and reached me in my little room of Time.

VI. Another form of proof is what might be called the mathematical. In plane geometry we live and move and do our thinking in a plane of two dimensions. In solid geometry we live in a world of length and breadth and height, which men call Space. But now Einstein and Bragdon come along to tell us that there is also a fourth dimension, which men call Time.

Let us imagine that the letters of the alphabet are two dimensional creatures living, say, on a flat piece of paper, with eyes capable of seeing nothing outside their flat domain. A pencil moving above them in space would be invisible until it pierced the paper. Then a great commotion would occur. The letters would gather around and exclaim, "What a cute little letter O!" Then as the pencil was pressed further in, from the point to the full cylinder the letters would exclaim, "How fast it grows!" Having attained its full maturity it would continue through the paper until in time it would complete its course and would be drawn out on the other side. As the little two-dimensional creatures would gather around the space it formerly occupied they would take out their handkerchiefs, weep a bit, and the pious would say, "Ashes to ashes, dust to dust"; the cynical would mutter, "Death ends all." How astounded they all would be if they were suddenly granted three dimensional eyes and could look upward and see the pencil in all its heighth and length and width and depth, whole, entire, and complete in the large spaces above them! We, too, were we granted suddenly higher dimensional eyes, would be amazed to know that our beloved had entered a larger dimension where the full length and depth of his being could be seen and realized and expressed in all of its completeness and beauty and perfection far better than in this little world bound within the limits of Time and Space.

VII. Finally, I have had amazing proof of immortality, not only in my own life, but in the lives of those I have been most closely associated with during the last twenty years.

I refer to something far greater than the fragrance of flowers that has come to me and others when talking of our loved ones, greater than voices, greater even than the inner mystic sense of communion that has brought precious comfort and inspired guidance to many. I am going now far beyond the senses and intuitions, to the cosmic powers that manifest in character and life over a long period of time.

In Dr. Buck's *Cosmic Consciousness* he explains that few men enter into a real experience of cosmic consciousness, that mystic sense of Oneness with the Father, until around the age of thirty-eight to forty-two. In their youth, most of them are not ripe for this experience. Around the fortieth year is the period when many of the great sages and seers, Isaiah, Jeremiah, Plato, and others, entered into this experience. That there are exceptions to this rule I have found in scores of college boys and girls hardly out of their teens, who have caught this vision. Imagine my surprise, however, when one day I took stock of college students who had caught this heavenly experience most profoundly and discovered that all of them had lost one or more members of their family.

My own spiritual growth began with the death of my twelve year old brother when I was fourteen. I felt that I must live the life for both of us and do the work of two men. All these years I have felt the help of his continuous partnership with me.

This linkage with heaven seems to release a power, at times an undimensional power, in the lives of those who have been left behind. Jesus proclaimed it when he said, "Greater works than these shall you do, because I go to my Father."

My mother died in 1922 and something celestial entered into my life. When the *Atlantic Monthly* described me as one who "finds prayer as natural as breathing, and whose every prayer is answered," I told my wife that I should write the editor that I had never made such an assertion as this. To my amazement she replied at once,

"Don't bother to write him. I have noticed that all your prayers have been answered since your mother died."

Then I remembered how my mother always wanted me to be a prophet rather than a statesman, a maker of men rather than a maker of money. But while she was in the body her wishes were limited in power by inhibitions of the human mind, and by tensions of the earth body. But the moment she was liberated from body tensions and mental limitations, her wishes became multiplied in power by infinity itself. That raised in me a great urge, and opened a great question: Why does one have to wait till he dies in order to give his prayers that power? Why cannot one die unto his little self now, and let his Great Self take control immediately? Why cannot he take an eraser great enough to erase himself completely out of the picture and let Christ shine through? Why cannot we here and now begin living in Eternity, and see the fulfillment of Christ's prayer, "Thy Kingdom come *on earth* as it is in heaven," and breathe our prayers to the Father in Heaven, knowing that they are infinite, unlimited, irresistible, even as they are infinite, unlimited, and irresistible in Heaven?

That I have done, at least that is what I have tried to do, and have seen the results in ways past finding out.

Jesus in his life and teachings demonstrated every one of these proofs of immortality. And then he crowned it all by actual mastery over death itself in its most terrifying and crushing form.

"Let not your heart be troubled: ye believe in God, believe also in me. In my Father's House are many mansions: if it were not so, I would have told you. I go to prepare a place for you. And if I go and prepare a place for you, I

will come again, and receive you unto myself; that where I am, there ye may be also."

This experience moved the greatest of his apostles to cry, "O DEATH, WHERE IS THY STING? O GRAVE, WHERE IS THY VICTORY?"